IS EVOLUTION BUNK?

IS EVOLUTION BUNK?

The science they did not teach you at school

MARTIN DOWN

Rehoboth

Media

Copyright © 2015 Martin Down

The right of Martin Down to be identified as the author of this work has been asserted by him in accordance with the Copyright, Designs and Patents Act 1988.

All rights reserved. Written permission must be secured from the publisher or the author to reproduce any part of this book, except for brief quotations in critical reviews or articles.

Published by Rehoboth Media

The Well Christian Centre
Swaffham Road, Ashill, IP25 7BT
www.fountainnetwork.org

Unless otherwise indicated, biblical quotations are taken from the New International Version (NIV) © 1973, 1978, 1984 by the International Bible Society.

ISBN 978-0-9574813-3-6

Cover design by MPH.

You are worthy, our Lord and God,
to receive glory and honour and power,
for you created all things,
and by your will they were created
and have their being.

Revelation 4:11

This book is a second edition of one that appeared in 2007 under the title *Deluded by Darwinism?* published by David C Cook. I never liked the title. The present, more provocative title, expresses more exactly my own thoughts and feelings on the subject.

Martin Down

CONTENTS

1	Is evolution bunk?	11
2	Theories	19
3	Faiths	25
4	In the beginning	31
5	Universal glue	37
6	Our earthly home	41
7	Water	47
8	Life itself	51
9	Irreducible complexity	57
10	Information	63
11	The story so far	69
12	Peppered moths	75
13	Pathways	81
14	The processes of change	87
15	The fossil record	93
16	Haeckel's embryos	99
17	Homology	103
18	A verdict on the evidence	107
19	The sedimentary rocks	113
20	Catastrophe	119
21	The flood	125
22	Mount St Helens	131
23	The young Earth: 1	135
24	The young Earth: 2	139
25	What do scientists think?	145
26	What do the Christians think?	151
27	The Creator	155
28	Suffering and redemption	159
29	The reappearance of God	163
30	Final thought	169
	Booklist for further reading	171
	Acknowledgements	173
	Index	175

1

IS EVOLUTION BUNK?

Let me tell you my story. At school I was taught to believe in evolution. When I was about 12 or 13 our biology teacher presented us with the evidence to support Darwin's Theory of Evolution. We were taught about Darwin's voyage in the *Beagle* to the countries of South America, about his observations of the finches on the Galápagos Islands, and of how he had been led to formulate the theory of the 'origin of species by means of natural selection'.

I remember some of the examples that we were given of how natural selection worked. There were the peppered moths. The original form of this moth was coloured so as to resemble the lichen-encrusted tree bark on which it rested. But during the Industrial Revolution the bark of these trees became blackened by soot and a new variety of the moth, much darker in colour, evolved. The lighter-coloured moths were more easily seen on the sooty trees by their predators and were eaten, while their darker-coloured brethren were better camouflaged and survived: natural selection and the survival of the fittest.

A second strand of the evidence for evolution was provided by Haeckel's embryos. Haeckel had drawn the embryos of various creatures at different stages of their development. By comparing human embryos with the embryos of other creatures, such as fish, amphibians, birds

Is evolution bunk?

and mammals, Haeckel showed that we all recapitulate the evolution of the species in our mother's womb; we all pass through an embryonic stage at which we look like a fish, a tortoise, a pig and a rabbit, before we become fully human.

Then there was the fossil record. Rocks lie in layers or strata all over the Earth. The lowest strata were laid down first and are therefore the oldest, the higher strata later and therefore more recently – the whole process, however, taking unimaginable aeons of time. Each layer in this geological column contains fossils, and the fossils show the slow and gradual evolution of the species. In the lowest levels the only fossils are those of trilobites and other primitive creatures. As we climb the column we come upon the fossils of fish, reptiles, birds and mammals, up to monkeys, apes and finally humans.

Another set of drawings in our biology textbooks also showed convincing evidence of evolution from a common ancestor (see p.13). There were undoubted similarities between the bones of a human arm and hand, a bat's and a bird's wing, a horse's leg and a porpoise's flipper. These all looked like variations of a single basic structure which had evolved by adaptation to different uses and environments.

Darwin's theory of the evolution of the species was only one part of a larger picture. When I was at school there was still a debate amongst scientists about the origin and age of the universe. Some like Fred Hoyle held that it had existed forever in a steady state, a theory which required the continuous creation of matter; others believed that all the matter in the universe began with a big bang and had been expanding ever since. Since my school days the question has apparently been settled in favour of the Big Bang. Today there is a general consensus that at some time about 13.7 billion years ago, the universe started with a big bang, out of which formed the stars, in which formed the higher chemical elements, out of which at some point and

Is evolution bunk?

somewhere in the universe came life, and from which evolved on Earth all the species of plants and animals which we now see (and many more which have since become extinct).

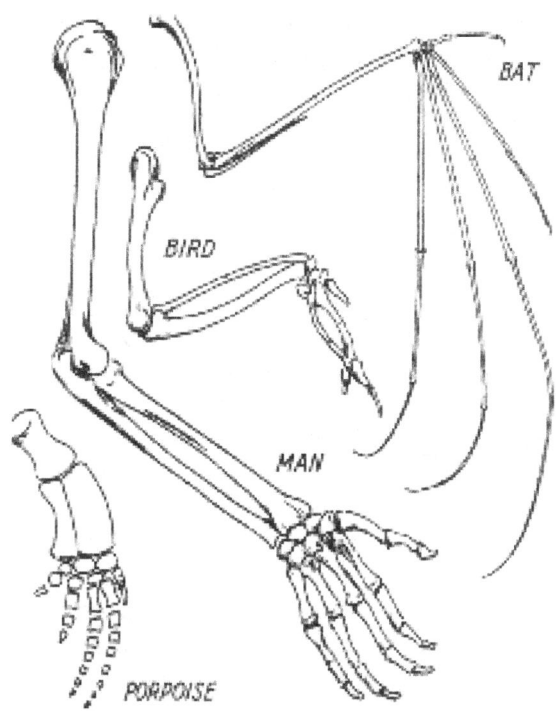

For the purposes of this book I will sum up all these theories under the title of 'evolution'. The connection between them is that they all presuppose a universe that has evolved by purely natural causes without any intervention by a supernatural agent or Creator God.

Is evolution bunk?

Like millions of other children of my generation, this was the story that I was taught and which I therefore believed. Teacher said it was true, and produced what seemed to be convincing evidence. After all, Teacher was supposed to know, and Teacher certainly knew more than my classmates and I did, so we believed it. What else could we do? And ever since, the story has been repeated and apparently confirmed by television programmes and books exploring the natural world, and by the announcement of ever more discoveries and breakthroughs in the world of science presented on the nightly news. No one who has lived through the last century and into this one has escaped indoctrination into the theory of evolution. Many people today have the impression that science has disproved the existence of God, or at least made belief in God redundant.

At school I went on to study the natural sciences, mainly physics and chemistry, up to the level required for entrance to Cambridge University. At that stage in my education I changed subject (but that is another story). But from school I learned at least the framework of the scientific method and of the scientific understanding of the universe in which we live, and since then I have taken as intelligent an interest as I can in the advancements of science, and especially as these have had a bearing on the question of origins, the origin of the universe, the origin of the Earth, the origin of life and the origin of species, including human beings.

* * *

I was also brought up in a Christian home and in a church. In neither do I remember the subject of creation and evolution ever being discussed – which itself tells a story about the nervousness or fear with which the church has

Is evolution bunk?

reacted to the theory of evolution for at least 150 years. At the age of 20, partly as a result of being persuaded at school of the truth of evolution, I would have described myself as an agnostic. But then I had the shattering experience, for an agnostic, of being addressed by the living God. I wrestled with this God for two years, before I finally gave in to him and became a Christian, professing for myself the faith that my parents and church had laboured to impart to me as a child.

When I became a Christian however I faced a dilemma: the theories of a naturalistic evolution of the universe and life which I had been taught at school told a very different story from the one I read in the Bible. Which was I to believe? There did not seem to be any option but to believe in the theory of evolution. Everyone believed in it and it seemed incontrovertible. I knew that there were Christian fundamentalists who believed in creation simply because the Bible said so, but it seemed to me that they did so at the expense of their intellectual integrity as people of the scientific age. (I would estimate them rather differently today.) But I had read the story of Galileo.

Galileo studied the stars through his telescope and as a result of his observations became convinced of the truth of the theory of Copernicus that the Earth and the planets revolved around the sun. The Pope condemned this theory on the grounds that the Bible said it was the sun which ran about in the heavens, not the Earth. In his defence Galileo invited one of his opponents, the professor of philosophy at Padua University, to look through the telescope and see for himself the evidence on which his conclusions had been based. The professor refused, and Galileo was condemned by the Inquisition. Christian fundamentalists seemed to me to be the followers of the Pope, refusing to look through the telescope or microscope at the evidence. Christians should not be caught in that trap again.

Is evolution bunk?

So for many years I modified the way in which I understood the Bible; I would have been described then as a Christian Evolutionist. Those stories at the beginning of the book of Genesis were merely poetical, the sort of stories that you might tell to children. To be sure, I believed that in some sense the world was God's creation, but I used to say that evolution was the glove that concealed the hand of God at work creating the world. Others I knew held more closely to the biblical account, but extended the six days of creation into ages or aeons. Billions of years could thus be accounted for within a biblical framework. In this way I lived with the apparent conflict between science and the Bible for over 20 years, vaguely uncomfortable with the compromise, but not able to see any alternative.

My eyes were opened in a new way in 1987 by reading, not the Bible, but a book by an Australian molecular biologist called Michael Denton, entitled *Evolution: a Theory in Crisis*. It was one of those revelatory moments when I saw for the first time, like the small boy in Hans Christian Anderson's fairy tale, that the Darwinian emperor, if not completely naked, was indecently exposed. I did not understand many of the details in the book, but I understood the main point: the evidence for the theory of evolution was no longer unchallenged or unchallengeable. In a very careful and detailed way a professional scientist, who was not even a Christian, was telling us that the theory of evolution was in trouble.

I have continued to read books like this, both in the physical and biological sciences, and it has become increasingly clear to me that the advancements of modern science are explaining, not more and more, but less and less, of the world around us. I had not been told the whole story at school, and popular presentations of science in the media had not been telling us the whole story since.

Is evolution bunk?

Not only are there major difficulties with the current theories of origins, from the origin of the universe to the origin of species and the origin of the human race, but also there is serious scientific evidence that God does exist and that the theory of God as the Maker of heaven and earth provides a more reasonable explanation of the world in which we live than the current atheistic orthodoxy. In this book I have tried to set out both the problems with the current orthodoxy and also evidence that points to the existence of God.

So is evolution bunk? Or do we need another theory altogether?

Is evolution bunk?

2

THEORIES

It is important to understand how science works. The first task is to make observations and measurements, to collect data. Out of these data the scientist constructs a theory which attempts to explain and account for the data. He then devises experiments to test the theory, experiments which can be repeated and verified by himself and by others. These experiments involve making more observations and measurements, collecting more data, which will help either to prove or to disprove the theory.

Strictly speaking, the theory can never finally be proved or disproved, because further research might always produce new data that would either invalidate an accepted theory or give new life to a discarded one. Indeed, in the view of Karl Popper, a great 20th century philosopher of science, it is essential to a scientific theory that it should be falsifiable. But in time the accumulation of data on one side or the other is usually such that a theory is accepted, at least for practical purposes, as proven. But in the end there is always something tentative and provisional about scientific theories, including the theories of physical and biological evolution.

Consider, by way of example, the law of gravity. It is said that the law of gravity was discovered by Sir Isaac Newton while sitting in a hammock under an apple tree in the garden of his home at Colsterworth. An apple fell on his

Is evolution bunk?

head, and he began to wonder why. The original observation was that the apple fell on his head. From this he formulated the theory that every body in the universe is attracted towards every other body by the same force, the force of gravity.

The two bodies concerned in the garden at Colsterworth were the apple and the Earth. Newton went on to devise a mathematical formula for calculating the force of gravity. Newton's theory was supported by an observation that Galileo had made from the leaning Tower of Pisa, an observation which goes against common sense, that the rate of fall of a body is constant, independent of its mass: a big apple and a little apple fall at the same rate. Newton's formula was found to describe the motions of the planets round the sun, and is used today to calculate the orbit of satellites round the Earth. In the twentieth century Newton's law was modified by Einstein's theory of relativity, but for ordinary terrestrial purposes Newton's law is still sufficient. In a similar way, Darwin observed the variation of the finches on the Galápagos Islands and formulated the theory of evolution to account for the origin of species. Darwin realised that his theory would have to be tested by further observation and experiment, but there is a problem with the theory of evolution.

Whatever happened in the past, it happened a long time ago; it cannot be observed directly or measured, and it can never be repeated: we cannot rerun the history of the world. In that sense, we cannot experiment with the theory of evolution in the same way that we can experiment with dropping apples on people's heads. The only way to test the theory of evolution is to collect more data from the world as we know it now, and see whether this tends to confirm or disprove the theory.

Until perhaps 30 or 40 years ago, it might have been said that research continued to confirm both the Big Bang

Theories

theory of the universe and Darwin's theory of the evolution of the species, but recently more and more evidence has appeared which has begun to throw these theories into doubt. There are now new facts to be considered and new evidence to be evaluated, facts and evidence that these old theories are finding it increasingly difficult to accommodate. But what is the alternative? That is the question which the scientific establishment is now facing.

There is an alternative to hand, and it is an alternative which only involves going back to a theory or view of the universe which scientists and everyone else took for granted until the nineteenth century: let us call it the theory of creation. It is the story which the Bible tells, a story generally thought to have been discredited, but a story which is perhaps now worth revisiting. Let us not get hung up on the details, but let us examine it broadly as an alternative explanation of the world that we see. Let me outline the theory like this:

> There is a God. By his word the universe was made. He spoke and it was done. He created light. He created the sun, moon and stars. He created the Earth. He created the land and the sea. He created fish to swim in the sea and birds to fly in the air, each according to its kind. He created the plants and the trees. He created the animals each according to its kind. Last, he created man. He did all this in a short period of time, say, a week, and not so long ago, say, less than 10,000 years. What God created was good, and for a while peace and harmony reigned on the Earth. Then something went wrong, and gradually everything fell apart. Fear and suspicion reigned on the Earth; animals and people started to kill each other; disease and death ruled the world. So God

Is evolution bunk?

decided to start again. He sent a worldwide flood, breaking up the crust of the earth, releasing water from under the earth, where it was held in subterranean reservoirs, and water from the atmosphere, in the form of rain. A man called Noah and his family, together with specimens of all kinds of creatures, survived the flood in a large boat, and from them the world was repopulated, say, 5,000 years ago.

Regard this as a theory, an alternative starting point from which to examine the data in the natural world around us. In this book we are going to examine some of the evidence and see which theory better fits the facts. Think of it, if you will, as a debate: a new debate between old theories, the theory of evolution and the theory of creation; or in more modern terms, a debate between two ideas of what accounts for the world in which we live, *chance or design*. Whether we like it or not, this debate is in progress. I hope that this book will help more people to understand what it is all about, and in particular to understand the arguments for intelligent design, arguments which many people, including me, now find more convincing than chance as an explanation of the world.

Many of the scientific questions that were once regarded as closed are, in an extraordinary way, now opening up again: the origin of the universe, the origin of life, the origin of the species, the geological history and the age of the Earth. The debate will continue for some time, probably many years, before there is any sort of new consensus, and perhaps there never will be. At present each side can make points to which the other side has difficulty responding. On each side scientists are working on their own theories. The evolutionists have been working on theirs for 150 years and large sums of money have been spent, and still are

Theories

being spent, on finding fresh evidence. Rockets are being sent to Mars and to Jupiter and guided into the path of comets and asteroids in order to support the idea that life evolved in space (see below, chapter 8). The universe is being scanned for signs of life on other planets, the Search for Extra-terrestrial Intelligence (SETI), to prove that what evolved on Earth evolved elsewhere too. And that is not to mention the vast sums spent on building and operating that modern Tower of Babel, the Large Hadron Collider at CERN.

The creationists have not had the big bucks that have been available to the evolutionists, but it is often the evolutionists' research that is advancing the case for creation. But then there is another factor which comes into the equation, and that is faith.

Is evolution bunk?

3

FAITHS

Whenever an item of television news concerns some scientific or medical breakthrough (at least once a week), the pictures over the reporter's voice invariably show a white-coated scientist peering down a microscope, surrounded by all the hi-tech paraphernalia of a modern laboratory. The image conveyed is of people engaged in an impersonal and dispassionate search for the truth and for the advancement of the welfare of mankind. Over on the other channel, however, there is probably another sort of drama, set in a hospital casualty ward or a forensic science laboratory, in which the same white-coated doctors and scientists take off their white coats and often quite a lot more, and engage in other activities of a very passionate and personal nature.

This should remind us that scientists are human like the rest of us, each with their own set of emotions, dilemmas, beliefs and prejudices. They are no more immune than the rest of us to the temptations of the world, the flesh and the devil, and they bring all this personal baggage into the laboratory, just as the rest of us bring it into the home, the school, the office, the pub or the shop. This is not to say that there is no such thing as objectivity and objective truth. There is, and we should all strive after it, but objectivity and objective truth are not the only factors in scientific research.

Is evolution bunk?

There is the question of what is researched in the first place. We have seen how scientists proceed. The first areas of subjectivity lie in what is observed and measured, and what theory or line of enquiry is then proposed for investigation. A pharmaceutical company, for example, is more likely to research a cure for Alzheimer's disease than for malaria. A cure for malaria would benefit more people than a cure for Alzheimer's disease, but it would not benefit the company so much: people who suffer from malaria are mostly poor and cannot afford expensive drugs.

Then there is often an element of subjectivity in the selection and presentation of results. Benjamin Disraeli is reported as saying, 'There are three sorts of lies: lies, damned lies and statistics.' We all know the difference between the people for whom the cup is half full and the people for whom it is half empty. Likewise, in presenting a new drug to the doctors the pharmaceutical company may emphasise that '50% of patients trialled experienced complete cure'. If they are honest they will also reveal what happened to the other 50%, but it might be in small print at the bottom of the page: 'Other patients died appalling deaths screaming in agony.' On the other hand, the lawyer suing the pharmaceutical company on behalf of the others will select and present the statistics in another way. These are no doubt exaggerated examples, but they illustrate how the common temptations of money and profits can influence the business of scientific research.

There have been well-documented examples in recent years of how the system of peer review in scientific journals has been used to suppress the publication of unwelcome data, data that failed to support the current orthodoxy, for example in the contentious area of Climate Change. There are other examples of scientists, who dared to espouse unpopular causes, finding their ascent up the career ladder blocked, or even finding themselves kicked off the career ladder altogether. The fact is that white-coated scientists peering into microscopes or staring at computer screens are no more immune from the pressure to conform than the rest of us. So we have to be aware of the subtexts of scientific debate as much as of the text itself, and when the debate is about evolution and creation the subtext is faith: something which motivates people even more powerfully than money or professional success.

A common charge brought against creationists is that their approach to natural history is influenced by their faith. Of course it is. But the truth is that the approach of evolutionists is also influenced by their faith. The theories of physical and biological evolution are an attempt to account for the natural world without God. They are an expression of naturalism: the pre-determined belief that the only form of reality is the physical one. Anything that is not physical, and cannot therefore be investigated and measured by the scientific method, is not real or does not count.

Evolution sets out to demonstrate that the world is self-explanatory: everything can be explained without God by the operation of natural laws and of chance, the random collision of atoms and molecules and the random mutation of genes. There is no design and no purpose, no Creator and no Judge; God and creation are hypotheses that we do not need. Evolution is both the child of atheism and, in the hands of people like Thomas Huxley and Richard Dawkins, a powerful weapon in the armoury of atheism. But atheism is a faith. It is as much an act of faith to believe that God does not exist as it is to believe that he does. The reality of a spiritual being, who is not by definition susceptible to scientific investigation, must be a matter of faith, one way or the other.

Science itself is the enterprise of discovering natural explanations for the phenomena of the world around us. A

Is evolution bunk?

scientist, whatever his faith, puts aside the idea of supernatural causality when he enters the laboratory; his job is to find natural causes. But the fundamental question is precisely this: is there more to life than science can explain? To rule out the possibility of supernatural causation from the start, as naturalism does, is to make a dogmatic statement of faith, and begs the very question that we are trying to answer: is the natural world self-explanatory?

I am a Christian; I believe in God. I believe in God not because science has proved that God exists, but because I have met God and know him personally. I am therefore biased (and you can underline that in the book right now). I want and expect to find evidence in the natural world of the handiwork of the God in whom I believe. But evolutionists are biased too. Darwin's religious doubts, which began early in his life, became a profound scepticism after the death of his beloved ten-year-old daughter Annie. One pities him. But the theory of evolution is the outcome of a scientist looking for an explanation of the phenomena of the natural world without God. David Attenborough, the man who through his television programmes has probably done more than anyone else to popularise the theory of evolution, is also an atheist. The reason he gives is not that the evidence for evolution is compelling, but that he cannot believe in a God who created a world in which there is so much suffering. Now that is a serious issue, the relationship between a good God and a suffering world, but it is not a scientific issue – it is a faith issue.

Richard Dawkins accuses Christians (and others) of 'fundamentalism': a dogmatic belief in God and in creation that ignores the scientific evidence. But, in spite of his claims to the contrary, Richard Dawkins is himself a fundamentalist of a different stripe: for him supernatural causation is fundamentally inadmissible as an explanation of anything, because God does not exist. If we come across some event or phenomenon in the natural world for which we cannot account in naturalistic terms at the present time, if there is an apparent gap, that is to say, in the chain of natural causality, he regards that only as a challenge for the scientists of the future; given time, Dawkins believes, we shall be able to find a naturalistic explanation for everything. But that is a faith position, and one that rests on a preconceived, dogmatic belief: there is no God.

The controversy over the theory of evolution has often been presented as a conflict between science and religion. That is not the case. A conflict there is, but it is the conflict between one faith and another, between theism and atheism, between belief and unbelief. Science is, however, intensely relevant to this debate. If the world is indeed God's creation, then there should be signs of this all around us. The Bible says, 'the heavens declare the glory of God' (Psalm 19:1), and, 'the whole earth is full of his glory' (Isaiah 6:3). If that is so, we ought to be able to see it in science. On the other hand, if we cannot see the hand of God in the world at all, if chance is sufficient to explain everything in the world, then we had better face up to the question of the ungodly, 'Where is your God now?' Science can help us to answer the question: is the world self-explanatory?

There was a time, as the theory of evolution gained ground, when believers took refuge in 'a God of the gaps'. There appeared to be gaps in the evolutionary process, and believers were only too pleased to plug the gaps with God. As science advanced, however, the gaps seemed to be getting smaller, and believers hurried to pull God out of the gaps before he was squeezed out altogether. It did not seem to be a very dignified place for God to be anyway, merely a stop-gap. However, today the truth is different. As science has advanced the gaps have become not smaller, but bigger and bigger. It would not be too much to say that

Is evolution bunk?

the various theories of evolution are now more gaps than theory.

So let us proceed to look at some of the evidence together. That was Galileo's challenge to the pope. In the seventeenth century the pope's man was not willing to look through the telescope lest the evidence destroyed his faith. We must all be prepared to look through the telescope or the microscope, evolutionists as well as creationists, and see what we see.

Charles Darwin himself at the beginning of *The Origin of Species* wrote: 'There is scarcely a single point discussed in this volume on which facts cannot be adduced, often apparently leading to conclusions directly opposite to those at which I have arrived. A fair result can be obtained only by fully stating and balancing the facts and arguments on both sides.' I could not have put it better myself. Unfortunately, neither Darwin, as he later acknowledged, nor his evolutionist successors, have ever done it. They still ignore or suppress facts that are inconvenient to their theories. This book is an attempt to state some of the facts on the other side, facts that lead to an entirely different conclusion, facts that they did not teach you at school.

4

IN THE BEGINNING

The conventional wisdom today is that the universe began with a Big Bang. At some time in the past all the matter and energy in the universe existed in an infinitely dense clump of indefinite size and shape. This 'clump' then exploded in all directions at once, and that was the beginning of everything. If there was anything before the Big Bang we would never be able to find out about it. The scientists call it a singularity, because it is a point at which all the present laws of nature break down and become inoperative. So, for practical purposes, we had better forget about it.

There are then other questions, to many of which there are, as yet, no clear answers. The universe has been expanding since the Big Bang, but will it go on expanding forever, or will it one day begin to collapse again? The present wisdom is that the former is the case. If the latter is the case, then the universe would end up in another singularity, the Big Crunch, and perhaps the whole cycle would start over from the beginning. But again, we would never know: any such future Big Crunch would be the end of the universe as we know it, and we cannot know if there will be anything after it, so we had better forget about that too. This universe is all we know and all that we have to explore.

As an example of the essentially provisional nature of scientific theories, it now seems possible that even the

Is evolution bunk?

theory of the Big Bang may have to be revised. The sums simply do not add up: if this now-conventional model of the universe is true, then there is a vast amount of both matter and energy missing: approximately 96% of the Big Bang universe is not there. At present scientists are calling what is not there dark matter and dark energy, meaning that it is energy and matter which we cannot see or detect in any of its usual forms. This begins to sound like fairies at the bottom of the garden: things we cannot see but nevertheless believe are there, by faith or wishful thinking.

For some years now scientists have been trying to find dark matter. The most advanced detector is at the bottom of a disused gold mine in South Dakota. Its aim is to detect particles of dark matter passing through a tank of inert gas cooled to -100°C. So far, no trace of dark matter has been found. Since 85% of the matter in the universe is 'dark' it seems remarkably elusive. As for dark energy, no-one has any idea how or where to start looking; no-one even knows what the concept might mean.

If I had a theory that failed to account for 96% of the universe, I might begin to think I needed a new theory. In an interview shortly before his death in 2012, the astronomer Sir Bernard Lovell admitted, "Twenty years ago we thought we knew almost everything about the universe; today we realize that we know almost nothing."

But whatever the outcome of the search for dark matter and dark energy, and whatever the implications of this for the theory of the Big Bang, there is a still more fundamental question which all cosmologists find themselves asking. Stephen Hawking, in his popular but incomprehensible book *A Brief History of Time*, talked about a universe without boundaries of space and time, and about imaginary time. Most of us find it hard enough to get a grip on real time, never mind imaginary time. But even Stephen Hawking finishes his book with the following words:

In the beginning

"What is it that breathes fire into the equations and makes a universe for them to describe? The usual approach of science of constructing a mathematical model cannot answer the question of why there should be a universe for the model to describe. Why does the universe go to all the bother of existing?"[1]

In a similar vein the astronomer Martin Rees writes: "Theorists may someday be able to write down fundamental equations governing physical reality. But physics can never explain what breathes fire into the equations, and actualizes them in a real cosmos. The fundamental question of 'Why is there something rather than nothing?' remains the province of the philosophers."[2]

But if that is so, then we must all be philosophers, because this fundamental question remains the most important of all, not to be shrugged off or dismissed as too high for us. Every man, woman and child wants to know where we come from and why we are here. When all is said and done, we are no further forward in answering those questions with all our scientific knowledge than our ancestors who sat beside their tents under the stars and wondered who made the world. For all the scientific research and the mathematical equations, the question of why the universe exists at all is still there and still demands an answer. The existence of the universe is not self-explanatory.

The nature of the universe is no less mysterious. When the atom was understood to be the smallest particle of matter, it was still possible to imagine it; we are familiar with iron filings – iron atoms are just extremely small iron filings. But when Rutherford split the atom into electrons,

---

[1] Stephen Hawking, *A Brief History of Time*, Bantam Press, 1988, p. 174.
[2] Martin Rees, *Just Six Numbers*, Weidenfeld and Nicholson, 1999, p. 131.

Is evolution bunk?

protons and neutrons the only way to imagine an atom was as a tiny solar system encircled by tiny planets. Now, scientists have 'split' even these subatomic particles into even tinier and more mysterious particles: quarks, muons, gluons and puons, for example, (I may have made the last one up). Most recently they have identified a Higgs boson, whatever that is. The point is that no-one has any means of grasping what these particles are: particles of what? When all is said and done, again we are no further forward in answering the question of the nature of the universe than our ancestors, who sat beside their tents under the night sky; they wondered, what are the sun, the moon and the stars? We wonder, what are muons, gluons and bosons; and we have no more idea than they had.

Because we have discovered so much we have persuaded ourselves that we have solved the mysteries of the universe. We have not. All we have managed to do is to reach the outer limits of our understanding, only to find that we are no nearer to answering the really important questions about the cosmos: who made it and out of what?

There are only two views that we can take. Either we can say that the question is unanswerable from a scientific point of view, which, as Martin Rees says, it is, and leave it at that. Or we can say that 'In the beginning God created the heavens and the earth' (Genesis 1:1). The first answer is no answer at all, just a refusal to look and think. The second answer is reasonable, compatible with science and deeply satisfying to the human soul. It corresponds to what we all feel and know, somewhere inside us, that however vast the universe may be, and however small we may seem to be in it, there is a meaning and a purpose to our existence and that meaning and purpose lies in the hand of God. The universe demands a First Cause and the First Cause is God.

In the beginning

There are, of course, those who will come back with the question, 'Then who made God?' To which the simple answer is, no one. God is not a being like all the other beings in the universe which demand a maker. God is spirit and, by definition, he is the One who is uncreated and the Creator of all things. Everything in the universe lives within the realm of change and time. The ancient Greek philosophers said, 'Everything changes,' and time is the result of change. But God never changes; he is the same from eternity to eternity. In him therefore there is no time; he is eternal. Out of his eternal changelessness he decided to create this universe of change and time. The day that he decided to do this was the beginning of time. He spoke and it was done. There is no better answer to the mystery of the universe than this one; indeed, there is no other answer at all.

Is evolution bunk?

5

UNIVERSAL GLUE

The universe is glued together by four fundamental forces. They are called the strong nuclear force, the weak nuclear force, the electromagnetic force and the gravitational force. The first two are the forces which hold the atoms themselves together, and we have no direct experience of them. The electromagnetic force has been experienced in one form or another by everyone who has had an electric shock, or by anyone who has ever pulled a magnet off the fridge – in other words, every two-year-old. But the gravitational force is the one with which we are most familiar in everyday life. Everyone who has dropped a plate or fallen off a bike has experienced gravity in a distressing way.

All these four forces have a specific and precise numerical value, which is constant throughout the universe. That is itself an astounding fact which seems to demand some sort of explanation: why is it that the universe is governed by such universal laws, laws which themselves make the practice of science possible? Einstein himself wrote, "The eternal mystery of the world is its comprehensibility ... The fact that it is comprehensible is a miracle."

Laws suggest a law-giver, and the observance of laws suggests a law-enforcer. It is not self-evident that the universe should exhibit this sort of consistency and

Is evolution bunk?

reliability. Indeed, before the dominance of a scientific paradigm of the universe, it was widely assumed that the operations of nature were capricious, and controlled, not by impersonal laws, but by the whims of gods and spirits. The modern practice of science has established that, generally at least, nature obeys unchanging laws. But this itself begs the question, why?

Even more astounding in the nature of the universe, is the fact that if any one of the four fundamental forces that hold the universe together were not precisely what it is, the universe would simply not work at all. The size of these forces is not self-explanatory: if the force of gravity were any stronger than it is, the universe would never have got off the ground in the first place, or if it had, it would have collapsed again as quickly as it had started. On the other hand, if the force of gravity were any weaker than it is, then everything in the universe would fly apart; nothing would stick together at all.

The same is true for all four fundamental forces and also for their relative sizes in relation to one another. For example, if the strong nuclear force were any weaker than it is, then the universe would be all hydrogen; if it were any stronger, the universe would have no hydrogen at all, and there would be no suns and no water. It is as if there were a set of heavenly dials which had to be set to exactly the right point before the universe began, if the universe were to work at all. It seems as if there was an unseen hand twiddling the knobs, and an unseen mind which calculated precisely at which point the dials should be set. As Fred Hoyle, an unbeliever, nevertheless said, 'A commonsense interpretation of the facts is that a super-intellect has monkeyed with the physics.'

There are other physical conditions and parameters that had to be just right before the world began, if it was to have any chance of existing. Roger Penrose, in a book called *The*

Universal glue

Emperor's New Mind, has calculated the degree of precision with which the universe has been created. Multiplying all the chances of error together, he demonstrates 'how precise the Creator's aim must have been'. Imagine a number, he says, with a lot of noughts on the end, not just a thousand (1,000) or a million (1,000,000), but 1,000,000,000 ... If you could put a nought on every atomic particle in the whole universe you would still not have managed to write down the degree of precision to which the Creator worked: i.e. 1 chance in 1,000,000,000.[3]

William Dembski devised a mathematical formula for deciding when a piece of Complex Specified Information could be a matter of chance and when it must be a matter of intelligent design. He makes the very conservative estimate that the lowest probability of a specified outcome being a matter of chance is 1 in 10^{150}, or 1 with 150 noughts after it. By this reckoning alone, the chances of the fundamental forces and conditions of the universe being what they are is so unlikely that it is off the scale altogether. It has to be a matter of design, intelligent design, and intelligent design requires an Intelligent Designer.

The only alternative to this conclusion is an idea which some scientists and mathematicians have suggested, called the 'multiverse'. This is the idea that there are, or were, a multitude of universes, each with a different set of values for the four fundamental forces and the original physical conditions. None of these universes actually works, except this one of course, so here we are!

This is not science; this really is fairies at the bottom of the garden, or universes at the bottom of the garden: we can never see them or communicate with them, but

---

[3] Roger Penrose, *The Emperor's New Mind*, Oxford University Press, 1989, pp. 343-4.

nevertheless we believe that they are, or were, there. But even if we were to accept the multiverse theory, we would still be left with the question of why did or do any of these universes exist at all; that question just got a whole lot bigger.

The precision of this universe is not self-explanatory; it demands some leap of faith, either a leap of faith into believing in a multitude of other universes, or a leap of faith into believing in God as the Designer of this one. The multitude of other universes are essentially unknowable. The God who made the world in which we actually live is essentially knowable, a God with whom we can interact, a God who makes himself known to us through the things which he has made, and who gives meaning and purpose to our lives.

6

OUR EARTHLY HOME

This chapter is going to read rather like the story of Goldilocks and the Three Bears. Whenever Goldilocks tried something belonging to Daddy Bear it was too hot, too high, or too hard. When she tried something that belonged to Mummy Bear it was too cold, too low, or too soft. Only when she tried something of Baby Bear's did she find that it was just right. We are going to look at the Earth and its place in the solar system from the point of view of its suitability for life, and especially for human life.

First, let us look at the sun. The sun is not just an average sort of star; it is a very special sort of star. Most of the stars in our galaxy are smaller than the sun, and are called red dwarfs; they give off red light and infrared radiation (heat), but not enough blue light and ultraviolet radiation to support life. Larger stars, however, for example F dwarfs, give off too much ultraviolet and blue light. Our sun is just right. Moreover, our sun burns very steadily. Red dwarfs are inclined to flare much more violently than the sun, so that their output of light and heat varies enormously from time to time. Our sun burns so steadily that its heat output is practically constant.

The Earth itself also happens to be in the right place in relation to the sun. As we shall see in more detail later, life on Earth depends on the presence of large quantities of water. Water is liquid only over a range of 100°C. Below

Is evolution bunk?

0°C it is solid ice; above 100 °C it is steam. Between those temperatures there is an even narrower band that is sympathetic to life; we all find it extremely uncomfortable if the temperature rises above 35 °C. The temperature of the Earth has to stay in a very narrow band in order to sustain life. If the Earth were nearer to the sun, it would be too hot and all the water would boil. If it were further away, it would be too cold and all the water would freeze. The temperature of the Earth and its distance from the sun have to be just right.

The Earth has an almost perfectly circular orbit round the sun. Orbits are not necessarily circular: elliptical orbits are just as possible. But an elliptical orbit would mean that the Earth would be much further from the sun at the end of its orbit and therefore much colder, and much nearer to the sun in the middle of its orbit and therefore much hotter.

This would mean that the temperature on Earth would vary too much. A circular orbit is essential. The Earth also rotates on its own axis, giving us the alternation of day and night. If the Earth did not rotate, one side would be permanently too hot and the other side would be permanently too cold. Again, the Earth has to rotate on its axis at the right speed. If it rotated too slowly, there would be too great a temperature difference between the night, when the Earth cools down, and the day, when it heats up.

The moon is also important to life on Earth. The moon helps to keep the Earth stable on its axis. The moon also creates the tides. The tides are important in flushing out nutrients from the rivers and increasing the ocean currents. The ocean currents are another important factor in stabilising the temperature of the Earth; they carry heat from the warmer equatorial regions to the colder arctic ones. But the moon has to be just the right size in proportion to the Earth and at just the right distance from the Earth. If the moon were any bigger or nearer, it would

Water

cause huge tidal waves and destabilise the Earth's motion. If it were any smaller or further away, it would not have any significant effect on the Earth. As it is, the moon is just right.

The atmosphere of the Earth is vital to life. A small body like the moon does not have sufficient gravity to hold on to an atmosphere at all; the astronauts have to carry their air in bottles on their backs. The Earth's atmosphere is composed of 78% nitrogen and 21% oxygen, both of which are vital to the life cycles of plants and animals. But the composition and density of the Earth's atmosphere are not self-explanatory.

Venus is a planet very much the same size as Earth, but its atmosphere is very different: it is composed of about 96% carbon dioxide and about 3% nitrogen, and atmospheric pressure at the surface of the planet is 96 times greater than atmospheric pressure on Earth. Mars, our nearest neighbour in the planetary system, has virtually no atmosphere at all and what there is, is 95% carbon- dioxide. Neither Mars nor Venus can support life. There are many factors which determine the nature of a planet's atmosphere, but the chief one is the planet's original endowment. Someone endowed the Earth with an atmosphere that was just right.

There are two more basic necessities for life on Earth: carbon and water. These two need to be present in abundance because carbon atoms are the essential building blocks of the molecules of life, and water is the essential medium of transport. But in addition life demands significant amounts of other elements, such as oxygen, nitrogen, iron, calcium and some 15–20 others. No other planet in our solar system has anything like the right chemical composition to support life, and in particular no other planet has anything like enough water.

Is evolution bunk?

The Earth is covered in vast quantities of water. We call them seas. Smaller quantities exist in lakes and rivers and ice caps. However, many forms of life on Earth, including human life, also depend on the existence of dry ground, and we cannot even take that for granted. If the Earth were much larger than it is, the increased downward pull of gravity would prevent the formation of mountains and hills. The Earth would be a much flatter place: there would not be much difference between the ocean beds and the mountain peaks. Indeed, it would be so flat that the whole Earth would be covered by the waters of the sea. We owe the dry land to the fact that the mass of the Earth is just right.

None of these facts is self-explanatory. They could all be otherwise. The sun could be bigger or smaller. The moon could be bigger or smaller, or not be there at all. The Earth could be bigger or smaller, or further from the sun, or nearer to it. The Earth could rotate faster or slower, or not at all. The Earth could have a very different chemical composition. Is it then all an accident, or does this mean something?

With their latest instruments astronomers are now searching the heavens for planets around other stars that might resemble the Earth. They are inclined to announce with a great fanfare that they have found 'twins' or 'lookalikes' of the Earth in other solar systems.

To take two of these recent announcements: there is a planet orbiting a small star in the constellation of Sagittarius near the centre of the Milky Way; astronomers have christened it OGLE- 2005-BLG-390Lb. However, this baby is five times as dense as the Earth, and is three times further from its star than we are from the sun. Its surface temperature is thought to be about −220 °C; not so much a lookalike as a feel-unalike. Another is called KOI-314C. This planet orbits a dim red dwarf at such a close distance

Water

that its surface temperature is thought to be around 104° C. If those are the nearest things that we have found in the universe to our earthly home, then it does appear that this planet of ours is something very special.

These are by no means the only examples that could be given of properties and conditions that have to be just right for the universe or life to exist. The physical properties of nature and of our planet in particular are not self-explanatory, and, like the properties of the fundamental forces of the universe, their combination would seem to be more than a matter of chance.

In *The Mind of God* Paul Davies writes, 'Through my scientific work I have come to believe more and more strongly that the physical universe is put together with an ingenuity so astonishing that I cannot accept it merely as brute fact.'[4] For those with the eyes to see, everything about the Earth has got intelligent design written all over it.

---

[4] Paul Davies, *The Mind of God*, Penguin, 1993, p. 16.

Is evolution bunk?

7

WATER

Water provides perhaps the most fascinating study of all. A substance, like water, has a whole range of physical and chemical properties; many of the properties of water are unique, and uniquely adapted to provide for the existence of life. Most substances expand with the heat and contract with the cold. Water is no exception, until it drops to 4 °C. At this temperature, just above freezing point, water as it cools starts to expand again, and as it freezes into ice it expands even more. This behaviour is without parallel, and it is essential for life. If water and ice continued to contract as they cooled, ice would form at the bottom of the pond or the sea instead of at the top. At the top it melts again as soon as the temperature rises. At the bottom it would never melt; it would build up year by year until the whole of the pond or the ocean was solid ice. However hot the surface became, only a shallow pool of water would form on top of the mass of ice, and life would be impossible.

Water plays an essential role in maintaining temperature stability, both on the Earth as a whole and also in the bodies of living creatures. It is uniquely suitable to do this because of two other properties which it has. Water absorbs a lot of heat – or, to put it another way, a lot of heat is required to raise the temperature of water, which is why it takes so long to boil the kettle. So the oceans absorb vast quantities of the sun's warmth and transport it round the

Is evolution bunk?

globe by means of the ocean currents, like the Gulf Stream. This way the temperature of the whole Earth is kept relatively uniform and stable. On the other hand, water plays an important role in helping us to preserve a uniform and stable temperature in our own bodies. Water absorbs even more heat as it evaporates; in fact, water absorbs more heat as it evaporates than any other fluid. So as we sweat and the sweat evaporates from our skin, our bodies lose heat and cool down.

Water is thin; it flows easily. Compare water with treacle, or even olive oil: it flows much more quickly. This is important in the circulatory system, which is based on water. If water were thicker, like treacle, the heart would have to work impossibly hard to pump the treacle through the veins in the body. There is another remarkable property of water. When it carries other cells in it, like blood cells, it flows even faster.

Our bodies are made up of 62% water. The weight of water in relation to the weight of other elements is another crucial property. If water were any denser than it is, we should not be able to stand up. If, on the other hand, water were any less dense than it is, almost every living creature, including the fish, would sink to the bottom of the sea or the lake. Every property of water seems to have been designed for the express purpose of supporting life.

Everywhere we look we see nothing but a remarkable string of coincidences that make life possible. It just so happens that the sun, the moon and the Earth are just the right size and in just the right place. It just so happens that there is an abundance of carbon and water and the other elements necessary for life on this planet. It just so happens that water has a whole set of unique properties which make it ideal to support life. It is not that just a few of these things have to be in place before life can begin; they *all* have to be in place. Is this chance or design?

Water

There are two ways of looking at this string of coincidences. It is rather like looking at one of those pictures which can be seen either as an old hag or as a beautiful young woman.

The picture does not change, but you can see it in two ways: some people see it one way and others see it the other. Which way do you see it? So we could look at the Earth and see its unique fitness for life and say, 'Well, it would be like that, wouldn't it? If all these things were not so, we would not be here to look at them. These are just the necessary conditions for life to exist.' You can say that it is all just a matter of chance: the strength of the four fundamental forces of the universe being exactly what they are is just a matter of chance; the properties of the Earth and the sun, of carbon and water, are just a matter of chance.

Is evolution bunk?

For most people, however, like Paul Davies (above), there comes a point at which they say, 'That is more than coincidence, more than lucky. That has to be design.' Michael Denton, in a second book entitled *Nature's Destiny*, sums up his conclusion: 'The cosmos is a specially designed whole with life and mankind as its fundamental goal and purpose, a whole in which all facets of reality, from the size of galaxies to the thermal capacity of water, have their meaning and explanation in this central fact.'[5] The whole cosmos is designed, and even designed specifically for human life, and therefore it has a Designer. And there are not many candidates for that role.

---

[5] Michael Denton, *Nature's Destiny*, The Free Press, 1998, p. 389.

8

LIFE ITSELF

Life is the ability of an organism to reproduce itself from within, to take in chemicals from outside and to use them to replicate itself. The basic unit of life is the cell. Most cells are so small that they cannot be seen with the naked eye. Yet they are far from simple. Television often shows a single cell being extracted from a group of cells under the microscope. The cell looks like a minute blob of jelly. But inside each cell is a truly astonishing world.

    Each cell is like a miniature city. It is enclosed by a wall all round it (called the membrane), but the wall has many gates in it through which goods are brought in and taken out. Inside the city there is the central square and the city hall (called the nucleus). In the city hall is filed all the information for the organising and functioning of the city (stored in DNA). From the city hall little messengers (mRNA) carry information to the factories (ribosomes) where hundreds of different proteins are manufactured. Proteins are complex chains made up by joining together anything between 50 and 1,000 amino acid molecules. It is like threading beads on a string. There are about 20 different amino acids used to build proteins, and they have to be joined together in special sequences to make different proteins. Proteins are the stuff out of which living things are built. There are thousands of different proteins. They are amazingly adaptable and complex; depending on

Is evolution bunk?

their composition, they coil, or fold, or are internally cross-linked. (But proteins are degraded at temperatures over 60 °C, which demonstrates the importance of temperature control on a planet that supports life.) Materials are transported round this cell-city on mini-trains (called the Golgi apparatus), and the whole city is powered by energy from mini-generators (called mitochondria).

Let Michael Denton describe the cell in his own way:

> Magnify a cell a thousand million times until it is twenty kilometres in diameter and resembles a giant airship. On the surface of the cell we would see millions of openings, like the port-holes of a vast space ship, opening and closing to allow a continual stream of materials to flow in and out. If we were to enter one of these openings we would find ourselves in a world of supreme technology and bewildering complexity. We would see endless highly organised corridors and conduits branching in every direction away from the perimeter of the cell, some leading to the central memory banks in the nucleus and others to assembly plants and processing units.
>
> We would see that nearly every feature of our own advanced machines had its analogue in the cell: artificial languages and their decoding systems, memory banks for information storage and retrieval, elegant control systems regulating the automated assembly of parts and components, error fail-safe and proof-reading devices utilised for quality control, assembly processes involving the principle of prefabrication and modular construction.

Life itself

> We would be witnessing an object resembling an immense automated factory, a factory larger than a city and carrying out almost as many unique functions as all the manufacturing activities of man on earth. However, it would be a factory which would have one capacity not equalled in any of our own most advanced machines, for it would be capable of replicating its entire structure within a matter of hours."[6]

And that is just a single cell, the simplest form of life! Evolutionists give the impression that all that is needed to generate life is a chemical soup, supposed to have existed on Earth long ago but unfortunately now off the menu, and a flash of lightning. The lightning is supposed to synthesise some amino acid molecules - and hey presto! - we have the building blocks of life. Never mind the idea of such a primeval soup, which is itself highly problematical – the description above of the simplest living organism, the cell, should be enough to show that a few amino acid molecules floating in a pond does not constitute life.

Fazale Rana, in a book called *The Cell's Design*, suggests that the minimum conditions for even the simplest prokaryotic cell to exist include several hundred protein-producing genes and an internal organization that can perform at least ten complex functions. The chances of all these factors assembling themselves by chance anywhere in the universe is infinitesimally small. Then there is the old riddle of which came first, the chicken or the egg? The theory of evolution has never been able to provide an adequate answer to this problem, and it reappears at every level of biological complexity. Within the cell, as Rana says,

---

[6] Michael Denton, *Evolution: A Theory in Crisis*, Adler and Adler, 1986, pp. 328–9, abbreviated.

Is evolution bunk?

'proteins can't be made without ribosomes and ribosomes can't be made without proteins'.[7] So which came first?

When Darwin wrote the *Origin of Species* in 1859 he could offer no explanation for the transition from inanimate matter to living creatures. Today, 150 years later, evolutionists are even further from being able to imagine, far less to demonstrate, how life began. The advances in our study of molecular biology and our knowledge of the living cell and how it works have put the origin of life as a matter of chance right off the map.

Some evolutionists have recognised the extreme improbability of life arising spontaneously from inanimate matter. The mathematician and astronomer Fred Hoyle famously compared it to the probability of a hurricane picking up the pieces in a scrapyard, whirling them round and leaving behind a fully functioning jumbo jet. The fact, as we all know, is that a hurricane picking up a jumbo jet would whirl it around and leave behind a scrapyard, not the other way round. Fred Hoyle, however, did not draw the obvious conclusion, but preferred to take refuge in the theory that life must instead have originated in outer space (panspermia). He realised that the possibility that so complex a mechanism as the living cell should have originated on Earth by chance was so small as to amount to an impossibility. But why should it be more likely that life should arise and survive in the inhospitable regions of outer space, than on this hospitable planet Earth?

In *The God Delusion* Richard Dawkins also admits the extreme improbability of life originating spontaneously on Earth, but then goes on to suggest that to believe in a God who created life is to believe in an even greater improbability. The logic of this is impenetrable. Let us say

---

[7] Fazale Rana, *The Cell's Design,* Baker 2008, the minimum conditions are found in ch.3, and the quotation is from p.108.

Life itself

we all acknowledge that the probability of a monkey typing the works of Shakespeare by chance is extremely small. Richard Dawkins then says that to believe that an intelligent being wrote them deliberately is to believe something even more improbable. Most people would conclude that we are forced to believe in Shakespeare, simply because we can read his works.

The living cell demonstrates two principles that are the keys to the theory of creation: that of intelligent design and that of irreducible complexity. We have looked at evidence for intelligent design already in the four fundamental forces of the universe. We have seen more evidence of intelligent design in the properties of water, and in the properties of the sun, the moon and the Earth itself. No more convincing evidence of intelligent design can be seen than the design of the living cell. Every little blob of jelly that you see being sucked into a tube under the microscope is a miracle of nano-engineering, smaller, more cunning, more reliable, more brilliant than anything invented or even imagined by mankind. The cell is an example both of intelligent design and of irreducible complexity.

Is evolution bunk?

9
IRREDUCIBLE COMPLEXITY

In order to understand the argument from irreducible complexity, we need to examine more closely the theory of evolution. As it is understood today, the theory of evolution relies on the chance mutation of genes. Mutations produce changes in the plant or animal that grows up in the next generation.

For example, scientists have produced in the laboratory a genetic mutation in the fruit-fly which results in the fruit-fly growing legs out of its head instead of antennae. Like a calf with two heads, this is a freak that in nature would quickly be eliminated. But evolutionists suggest that from time to time a mutation produces a change in the creature that is beneficial. If the change gives the mutant an advantage in the struggle for existence, then the mutation will be passed on and the species will evolve.

If we think of these changes in engineering terms, we could say that beneficial mutations correspond to improvements in the design of the machine. Never mind that most of the mutations we actually observe in nature are degenerative and not at all beneficial – the theory of evolution maintains that over long periods of time a whole series of beneficial mutations has led not just to the development of improvements in the species, but to the evolution of entirely new kinds.

Is evolution bunk?

The essence of the theory of evolution is that change must take place by means of a series of small steps, as one beneficial mutation is added to another. There cannot be any radical discontinuity in the chain of evolution. Therefore, if one species has evolved from another, or if a specific organ has evolved where there was none before, then this must have happened in a series of small steps, one step at a time. There are two problems with this theory, the first of which is summed up in the phrase 'irreducible complexity'. (We shall look at the other, 'evolutionary pathways', later.)

We have seen in examining the tiny world of the cell that at the microbiological level life is the functioning of millions of little molecular machines. Very often a function depends on the working of not just one little molecular machine, but several little molecular machines working together. In the chemical reactions studied by molecular biologists proteins often work together in teams. According to the theory of evolution, a single genetic mutation might lead to an improvement in the functioning of one of these little machines or one member of the protein team, but it cannot account for the evolution of several molecular machines or several proteins *together* which depend on one another to function at all.

Ariel Roth, in a book simply called *Origins*, suggests a comparison with a domestic burglar alarm system. The system consists of a number of sensors fitted to the doors and windows of the house which react if these are opened; the sensors are connected by electric wires to a central control panel which reacts to a signal from the sensors; the control panel is then connected by electric wires again to an alarm; the alarm reacts to a signal from the control panel by giving off a fearful shriek which frightens the burglar to death and wakes everyone around; the whole system has to be connected to a supply of power, which may be generated many miles away.

Irreducible complexity

Let us say that there are at least five elements to this system: the sensors, the wires, the control panel, the alarm itself and the power supply. Each of these elements is itself a complex machine requiring its own design and manufacture; there will be a separate set of drawings for each element, and they may be manufactured in separate factories. Over a period of time the manufacturers will probably introduce modifications to improve the design of one or more of these elements. For example, the sensors could be improved so that they were more unobtrusive to the incoming burglar, or more difficult to disable; the alarm could be improved to phone through to the nearest police station as well as emitting a fearful shriek; miles away the power might be generated by burning natural gas instead of coal.

All these improvements could take place and be incorporated into the system one by one. But the fact is that the system, improved or unimproved, will not work at all unless all the five elements are present, all are working at the same time, and all are connected together. If there are no sensors to detect the entry of the burglars, the system is useless. If the control panel has not yet been designed, the sensors cannot send any signal to the alarm. If the alarm is faulty, there is no deterrent to anyone breaking and entering. And even a perfect system will not work unless it is wired up and connected to a power supply. This is irreducible complexity.

It might be argued, and is argued in biological examples, that one element, such as the power supply in our own example, might be already present with another application, ready to be adapted to a new one. That does not change the underlying logic; our burglar alarm still needs at least four new elements which have no other previous presence in the house and which are useless without the others: the sensors, the control panel, the alarm and the wiring.

Is evolution bunk?

Everywhere you look in biology you see systems of irreducible complexity, not just here and there, but everywhere, and, unlike the burglar alarm system with five elements that we have just examined, biological systems often involve dozens of elements. In *Darwin's Black Box* Michael Behe describes a relatively simple biochemical machine called a cilium. A cilium looks like a tiny hair growing on the outside of a cell. It functions like a miniature oar or paddle. If the cell is stationary the cilia can move liquid over the surface of the cell; there are cilia in the windpipe which combine to move the mucus and expel any foreign bodies that we may have breathed in. On the other hand, if the cell is free to move, the cilia can propel it through the liquid like a little boat. Each such cell has up to 200 cilia or oars, like a biological galley. Each cilium is made up of about 200 different proteins, the use of many of which is still unknown. The principal working parts have been identified, however, and each part depends on some different marvel of molecular design.

There is a series of rods made out of a protein called tubulin; these are the loom of the oar. Next there are motors made of the protein dynein, which cause the oar to move. Third, there are links between the rods made of another protein, nexin, which cause the rods to whip back again. And lastly nothing would happen at all, as with the burglar alarm, unless there was a power supply and, as with the burglar alarm, the power supply comes from a different source altogether, the mitochondria.

For any complex biological system such as this to have evolved by natural selection demands that each and every element should have evolved in working order *at one and the same time*; nature does not have any use for spare parts sitting on shelves waiting to be used. But each element can only evolve in single steps through the random mutation of a gene. The cilium contains 200 proteins, which means that it depends on 200 genes.

Irreducible complexity

Each gene is the blueprint for one protein or one element of the cilium. A chance mutation in one gene might produce an improvement in one element of the cilium, but it is beyond the bounds of possibility that random mutations should have taken place in so many genes at one and the same time, so as to assemble a cilium that worked in the first place. Whatever the function of most of those 200 genes in a cilium, the proteins and the structure for the four basic elements at least, the rods, the motor, the links and the energy source, must all have come together at the same time for the machine to work at all: any one is functionless without the others.

Within the cell itself, there is one supreme example of irreducible complexity and intelligent design: the mitochondrion. Mitochondria are the little dynamos that power the living cell. Each cell contains DNA specific to the kind of creature to which it belongs. DNA contains the code for making all the proteins that the organism needs. The mitochondria, however, contain their own DNA; a mitochondrion is almost like a cell within a cell. This has led evolutionists to suppose that mitochondria were once separate organisms that became incorporated into the cells of other organisms to provide them with energy. But the truth is much stranger. For the mitochondrion does not contain the DNA for all its own proteins, but only for some: 13 out of 103.

In the DNA of the cell itself is the code for the other proteins that the mitochondrion needs, and the cell itself manufactures these proteins specifically for export to the mitochondrion. Neither the cell nor the mitochondrion can function without the help of the other; the relationship is irreducibly complex. From where would the cell get its energy without the mitochondria? How would the mitochondria reproduce themselves without the proteins from the cell to add to their own? Who tells the cell which proteins to produce for the mitochondria and which it can

Is evolution bunk?

produce for itself? Who programmed the DNA of the cell to produce the proteins that the mitochondria, not the cell itself, needs? The relationship between the living cell and the mitochondria is the most beautiful and elegant example of intelligent design and irreducible complexity.

The principle of irreducible complexity is fatal to the theory of evolution. Darwin himself admitted, 'If it could be demonstrated that any complex organ existed which could not possibly have been formed by numerous, successive, slight, modifications, my theory would absolutely break down.' Today the electron microscope, and the molecular interactions within living organisms which it has enabled us to observe, have demonstrated not that numerous, successive, slight modifications do not take place, but that for complex organs to have evolved, too many successive, slight modifications would have had to have taken place *simultaneously* for the idea to be plausible. On the principle of irreducible complexity, according to Darwin's own criterion, the theory of evolution absolutely breaks down.

10

INFORMATION

We live in the age of information technology. I am typing this book on a computer. I have very little idea how it works, but I have learnt the basic terminology and know enough to use it. I know that I have some hardware: it is a box under the desk, to which is connected this keyboard, and the box under the desk is connected in turn to a screen which I am watching as I type. The whole thing is connected up to mains electricity, and this system is itself a good example of irreducible complexity. I am also aware that the hardware by itself could achieve nothing. For me to use this computer I also need some software. This has been installed on the computer before I bought it, or I have downloaded it from the internet as I needed it. But someone somewhere has written this software so that I can use my computer to write this book.

The basic technology inside my computer is the silicon chip. I do not understand how this works either, except that the chip contains millions of electrical circuits which can be switched on or off by means of tiny switches. Everything works on the simplest possible code, the binary code. Everything is either a 0 or a 1; a 0 if a switch is off, a 1 if the switch is on. All the information on my computer is in code, a code consisting of a series of 0s and 1s. Morse code was a similar binary code: everything was encoded as either a dot or a dash. Each letter of the alphabet was

Is evolution bunk?

represented by a unique series of dots and dashes, so that SOS was represented by ••• – – – •••

DNA is similar to a computer; it is a form of information technology. The hardware consists of molecules of sugar and phosphate, joined together alternately in a very long chain. To each of the sugar molecules is attached one of four other molecules, the chemicals adenine, guanine, cytosine and thymine, indicated by the letters A, G, C, T (the phosphate molecules in the chain are simply links). These four letters are the code that DNA uses for storing information; just as the binary code is the code which the computer uses. But just as the hardware in the computer and the information stored in it are two completely different things, so the basic chemicals of DNA and the information stored in it are also two completely different things.

So far in this book we have been examining the hardware of life, the molecules of which everything is made, and their complex interactions which are similar to the workings of mini-machines. DNA is a major component in an astonishingly ingenious and elegant machine, as we have seen, the cell. How this machine could have come into existence by chance defies explanation. But in addition to this, the question of where the *information* contained in the DNA comes from also demands an answer. Someone had to make the hardware, then someone had to write the software, and then someone had to input the information.

To take another example, you are reading my thoughts in a book. The 'hardware' of the book is a sheaf of paper, glued together at the back, and ink printed in the shape of letters on the page. The code that we are using is a set of 26 letters, commonly called the alphabet, with occasional recourse to another code of ten digits, commonly called numbers. But the information that I am encoding for you is

Information

something of a different kind from the paper and ink on which it is written.

A random selection of these 26 letters would not convey anything at all. Occasionally random letters might spell a simple word like 'cat', but writing this book involves a conscious arrangement of these letters to convey what I want to say. The means by which information is stored and conveyed is one thing; the information itself is quite another. For you to have this book in your hands, someone had to print it, but before that, someone had to write it, in this case me.

A gene is a short length of the DNA chain which contains the coded instructions for building a protein. There are thousands of different proteins and each one requires between 1,000 and 2,000 digits of the four-letter DNA code to specify how to make it. Human DNA has about 3,000 million digits in all. This book, by contrast, contains a mere 150,000 characters. The immense sequence of coded digits in DNA did not come about by chance, any more than the sequence of letters that you are now reading came about by chance. (I can tell you that it took a lot of blood, sweat and tears, and what, for want of a better word, I call my mind.)

Every creature has its own specific DNA, indeed every individual has its own specific DNA. From its DNA both the individual and the species can be identified. There is human DNA and there is chimpanzee DNA, and there is haddock DNA, and there is worm DNA. The information for each species is contained in its DNA. DNA is the key to reproduction, to life. Without DNA even the simplest cell cannot reproduce, and life cannot begin. Until reproduction begins, the process of natural selection through the survival of the fittest, essential to the theory of evolution, cannot begin either.

Is evolution bunk?

The oldest question in the world, 'Which came first, the chicken or the egg?' now has an answer. DNA came first, then reproduction, then selection, and DNA came fully loaded with the requisite information to make life happen, whether it is chicken life or human life or chimpanzee life or haddock life. The question is, 'Where did all this information come from in the first place?'

Information means intelligence, a mind. Books do not write themselves. Computer software does not write itself. Microsoft or Apple may be able to invent computers which can write software, but those computers themselves had to be programmed by a human mind in the first place. Many of the processes on a car assembly line today are carried out by robots. Genes can be compared to little robots that carry out the processes required to build limbs and organs, but someone has to programme the robots on the assembly line before the line begins, and someone programmed the genes before life began.

Genetic mutations, on which the whole theory of evolution depends, are merely changes in the letters of a book. I am not a very good typist and I frequently make mistakes: I often type 'slef' for 'self'. In DNA that is a genetic mutation. Most of my mistakes and most genetic mutations make nonsense. My computer software identifies and corrects many of my errors automatically, and there are mechanisms in the cell which also correct many DNA copying errors automatically.

Just occasionally by chance I may mistype a word that does actually spell something else: I sometimes type 'form' instead of 'from'. In a sentence, this also usually makes nonsense, but occasionally a mistake may make sense, admittedly different from what I had intended, but perhaps, even more occasionally, it may make better sense than I had intended. So with genetic mutations, which are accidental changes in the genetic code: most of them make

Information

nonsense; very, very occasionally one may make something better than the original sequence did. That would constitute a beneficial mutation. But to suppose that a human being could evolve from a blob of slime by a series of DNA errors is the same as supposing that if I type enough errors into this book I shall end up writing *War and Peace* by mistake.

The writing of DNA did not happen by chance. DNA was written before life began. Like the writing of this book, writing DNA requires a mind. The fact is that, whichever way we look at the world, we see unmistakable signs of a superhuman intelligence.

Is evolution bunk?

11

THE STORY SO FAR

This is a good point at which to review our progress so far. We are looking at evidence, facts collected by science about everything from the physical laws that govern the universe to the molecular structure of DNA. We are then examining two theories to see which theory best accounts for the facts which we have seen: the theory of evolution or the theory of creation. The theory of evolution accounts for these facts, in a word, by the operation of chance.

As the French biochemist Jacques Monod put it, 'Chance alone is at the source of every innovation, of all creation in the biosphere; pure chance, absolutely free but blind, at the very root of the stupendous edifice of evolution.'[14] The theory of creation, on the other hand, accounts for the facts which we observe, in a word, as design, the work of God. This theory postulates that there is a spiritual being outside time and space by whose word, according to whose design, the visible universe and everything in it were made.

So let us see how these two theories meet the challenge of explaining the facts so far. We have examined the evidence in six areas of science. We have observed a number of facts which are not self-explanatory, and the purpose of our enquiry is to seek an explanation.

---

[14] Jacques Monod, *Chance and Necessity*, Collins, 1972, p. 110.

Is evolution bunk?

1. The very existence of the universe demands an explanation. As Stephen Hawking asked, 'Why does the universe go to all the bother of existing?' Or Martin Rees, 'Why is there something rather than nothing?'
2. Astrophysicists now realise that the fundamental physical conditions at the moment when the universe began, such as the values of the four fundamental forces, were extremely finely tuned. Mathematicians like Roger Penrose have calculated that the possibilities of this happening by chance are so small as to be absurd. So what other explanation is there?
3. The properties of the universe in our own locality are no less finely tuned to support life: the nature of the sun, the moon and the Earth itself, the physical properties of water and the other elements, and their distribution on Earth. If almost any of these things were different from what they are, life would not be possible. These coincidences require an explanation.
4. The origin of life itself requires an explanation. There is an enormous gap between animate and inanimate objects, between rocks and water and air, on the one hand, and trees and horses and people, on the other. The most primitive living cell is a marvel of ingenuity and complexity. How did it originate?
5. The life of all living organisms depends on the interaction of a multitude of little biochemical machines and processes. These processes and machines invariably interlock in such a way that one part has no value without the others. How did it happen that these different parts came into existence in the same place and at the same time together?

The story so far

6. Finally, the unraveling of the structure and mechanism of DNA has revealed an amazing, computer-like world in which the 'hardware' of chemical molecules store and transmit an astounding quantity of biological information. The question arises of the origin not only of the 'hardware', but also of the information.

So we now need to ask our two theories what answers they can give to our questions. Let us start with the *theory of evolution*.

1. Evolution offers no answer at all to the mystery of existence.
2. Evolutionists can only explain why this universe is viable by suggesting the theory of a multitude of universes, the 'multiverse' theory.
3. Evolution sees all the favourable coincidences of life on Earth as so much good luck. If we had not won the lottery, we should not be living on our winnings.
4. Evolutionists have no explanation of the origin of life.
5. Evolution can offer no explanation for the phenomenon of irreducible complexity. Richard Dawkins in *Climbing Mount Improbable* acknowledges that evolution seems an impossible mountain to climb on the sheer face of the side that we can see, but suggests that there must be gradual steps up it on the side that we cannot see.
6. Evolutionists can only suppose that things like DNA molecules and this book happen by chance.

Is evolution bunk?

Can the *theory of creation* do better?

1. Creation proposes that God is the Creator of the universe. The universe and everything in it owes its existence to his will and word.
2. For creationists there is no difficulty in explaining the fine-tuning of the universe. It was created by an intelligent and all-powerful God, who naturally chose the right conditions of the universe before it began.
3. Creation by God included the sun, the moon and the Earth itself, land and sea, and the properties of all the elements within them; each was carefully and deliberately designed to make life on Earth possible.
4. Creationists propose that God created all living creatures from the simplest living cell to the human being, not only designing them, but making them too.
5. Creation involves the supposition that each living creature was made complete according to its kind. All the irreducibly complex processes and machines in living organisms were assembled and put together by God at one and the same time.
6. Creation accounts for the information encoded in DNA as the product of the mind of God.

Perhaps we shall never reach the point where either theory is conclusively proved or disproved. Scientific theories always have a quality of tentativeness or provisionality about them. So there will always be room for each person to make his or her own choice. It comes down to a matter of faith. You can still believe in chance as the explanation for all things, if you want to do so. On the

The story so far

other hand, there is no scientific reason why you should not believe in God as the explanation of all things. You have to decide which explanation seems to you better to fit the facts and (in a word which mathematicians and scientists are not afraid to use) which theory seems to you to be the most elegant.

If you wish to adopt the theory that chance and the operation of purely natural causes accounts for the world in which we live and our own existence within it, then you will probably have to leave it to the boffins to test this theory for you. If, however, you wish to adopt the theory that God is the explanation of the universe, then you can go ahead and test this theory for yourself: you simply need to say, 'God, if you are there, please show me,' and see what happens.

I am open to the accusation that I have been cherry-picking the facts that suit my argument. Of course I have. Everyone has to select. No one can present or even know all the facts; there are simply too many of them. Everyone selects the facts that support his or her own case. No one does this more than the evolutionists. But it is now time for us to return to the facts which the evolutionists put forward to support their case. In the next few chapters we shall revisit those pieces of evidence which were presented to me as a schoolboy and which at the time persuaded me of the case for evolution. We shall look at what fresh light has been thrown on this evidence in the last 50 years, and some of the results will be surprising.

We then need to go on and look at the question of how old the Earth is. The theory of evolution requires the Earth to be exceedingly old; the received wisdom at the moment is that it is about 4.5 billion years old. The theory of creation, on the other hand, has no such requirement, and suggests that the Earth is relatively young, a matter of only a few thousand years old. We shall look at some of the

Is evolution bunk?

evidence that sheds light on this controversy also. Finally, we shall look at the question of who this Creator God might be, how we can know him and, yes, why there is so much suffering in the world.

12

PEPPERED MOTHS

Let us return to that primary evidence for evolution: the case of the peppered moth (p.11). There is some doubt about the validity of the observations that supported this argument. But, in any case, it was at best an example of variation within a species, *Biston betularia,* the variation between lighter and darker forms, not the evolution of a new species. There are many other examples of variation within species, but they also demonstrate the limits of variation. The bacterium *E.coli*, for example, has been extensively used to explore the mechanics of life. *E.coli* has the advantage of reproducing itself in half-an-hour. Its evolution over 1 million generations can be studied in 60 years, a task that for human beings would take at least 15-20 million years. *E.coli* has been bombarded with X-rays, exposed to different environments, and attacked with antibiotics. It has been observed mutating, absorbing viruses, and adapting to extreme conditions. It has been genetically engineered to produce pharmaceuticals for human beings. There are thousands of different strains of *E.coli*, some naturally, some artificially produced, yet they all remain strains of *E.coli*. At the end of all these experiments *E.coli* has never evolved into anything other than E.coli.[15]

---

[15] See Carl Zimmer, *Microcosm:E.coli and the new science of life.* Heinemann, 2008.

Is evolution bunk?

To go further we need to understand something of the way in which living organisms are classified. Biologists historically divided living organisms according to their internal and external characteristics. There are seven levels of classification: kingdom, phylum, class, order, family, genus and species. In biology all these are technical terms. For example, there is one *kingdom* of plants and another of animals. Within the animal kingdom there are *phyla*: molluscs, for example, which have a shell, like the snail; arthropods, which have an external skeleton, like beetles and spiders; and vertebrates, called chordates, which have an internal skeleton.

Within the phylum of chordates there are five *classes*: fish, amphibians, reptiles, birds and mammals. The characteristics which distinguish these five classes are hair (mammals), feathers (birds), dry scaly skin (reptiles), moist scale-less skin (amphibians), and fins and scales (fish). These and a few other characteristics are sufficient to assign every known animal to a class.

As more detailed characteristics are introduced, so the animal kingdom can be further subdivided into *orders*, *families* and *genera*. The smallest group in the classification is the *species*. A species is a group of organisms which resemble each other closely and which can interbreed to produce live offspring, which in turn can breed. Thus the pooch on the hearthrug belongs to the species *Canis familiaris*, the domesticated dog, of the genus *Canis*, of the family Canidae, which also includes the wolf, fox and jackal, which in turn is part of the order of Carnivora, or meat-eaters, which also includes the families of bears and cats.

The cat family, on the other hand, includes not only the ginger tom next door, but lions, tigers and cheetahs. It is the criterion of interbreeding that usually determines the limits of a species.

Peppered moths

Within each species, however, there are many variations. Indeed, every individual varies slightly from every other individual. Dogs have been bred for many different purposes and have come out in many shapes and sizes. The possible range of variations within a species is sometimes quite extraordinary. Dogs can range from the bizarre Pekinese to the huge Great Dane; they can be smooth haired or wire haired or curly haired, with floppy ears or pricked ears. But they are all dogs, and apart from difficulties of size they can all interbreed with one another. Their specialised breeding has been artificial: human beings have selected certain characteristics or qualities which are useful to them and inbred those characteristics to produce a breed.

What happened to the peppered moths was simply an example of selective breeding, brought about in this case not by human, but by natural selection. But the key point is that the changes we are talking about are only variations within a species; they are not the creation of a new species. The peppered moths changed, but they were still peppered moths. Dog breeders can breed dogs forever, but they can only produce dogs, not cats. Scientists have bred *E.coli* for ever, but they have only produced more *E.coli*.

It is possible that variation can continue far enough to produce in the end a new species. Darwin's explanation of the different species of finches and other birds that he observed on the Galápagos Islands, and on the basis of which he constructed the theory of evolution, is generally accepted as the right one: an original finch species migrated to separate islands and there evolved in different directions until the populations could no longer interbreed, and thus formed separate species or subspecies. But notice not just the fact, but the limits of the changes: the species differ in size, colour and the shape of the beak, just as dogs bred for human purposes vary in size, colour and shape of nose. But at the end of the day the

Is evolution bunk?

finches are still finches; they are not seagulls or bats; just as, at the end of the dog breeder's day, dogs are still dogs and not cats.

As we climb up the classification scheme more and more characteristics change, and more major ones too. As we go up the scale from species to families and from families to orders and from orders to classes, there is no observational evidence that one group has ever changed into another, and it becomes harder and harder to imagine that mere variation within species could produce such great changes. Darwin argued by extension that just as one species of finch had evolved into another species of finch, given enough time, anything could evolve into anything. But such an argument is fallacious.

Take bridges, by way of comparison. We are, after all, talking about bridging the gaps in nature between species, then between families, then between orders, and classes, between phyla and kingdoms. It was a great achievement of engineering when Thomas Telford built a suspension bridge in 1826 over the Menai Strait between Wales and Anglesey. A much longer suspension bridge was built in 1937 to cross the Golden Gate Strait in California. Darwin would have argued by extension from these two examples that, given enough time, a suspension bridge could be built from anywhere to anywhere. This is clearly fallacious. A suspension bridge cannot be built across the Atlantic Ocean; it even proved unfeasible to build such a bridge across the English Channel. It is not just a question of scale: the sort of problems that would have to be overcome to bridge the Atlantic are different from the sort of problems that have to be overcome to bridge a river or a strait. Scale itself does matter: there are limiting factors in the tensile strength of materials and the stresses due to wind and water. But more than this, a suspension bridge over the Atlantic would be absolutely impossible because of the curvature of the Earth.

Peppered moths

The gaps between species, for example between different species of finches, are not very great. The gaps between families, for example between dogs and cats, are greater. Nowhere have either nature or human beings been seen to be able to cross this gap. The gaps between orders, classes, phyla and kingdoms are bigger still. No bridging of these gaps has ever been observed, and indeed the problems are so great that bridging them, like bridging the Atlantic Ocean, is unimaginable. Darwin's error was to mistake *variation* within a narrow range of organisms for the *evolution* of all forms of life.

Someone who lived through the twentieth century would have observed the evolution of the motor-car, from the Model T Ford to the Ferrari F430 Spider. This development took place through a long series of small modifications over a long period of time: micro-evolution. (Ignore for the moment the fact that none of these modifications took place by chance, but were all the work of intelligent designers.) But it might be tempting to go further. In the nineteenth century the predecessor of the motor-car was the horse-drawn carriage. There are many likenesses between the two vehicles – wheels, seats, doors, windows, even lamps. So we might be tempted to conclude that the motor car had in fact evolved from the horse-drawn carriage: that by a long series of small modifications over a long period of time, the horse had evolved into an internal combustion engine. We do, after all, still talk about cars having horsepower! It did not happen.

Is evolution bunk?

13

PATHWAYS

No examples of evolution greater than those given in the previous chapter have ever been observed in nature; there are gaps in the forms of living organisms much greater than the gaps between species, and no one has actually observed evolution taking place across any of these gaps, nor discovered incontrovertible evidence that it has happened in the past. If the theory of evolution is to be sustained, either a series of intermediate forms which clearly bridge these gaps has to be found in nature, either in the form of living organisms or fossilized ones, or we have to be able to imagine at least a theoretical pathway by which the gaps might have been bridged even if the intermediate forms no longer exist. It is essential to this procedure that all the intermediate forms should have been fully functional in their own time and in their own way.

The problem is similar to a sort of word puzzle that is sometimes found in magazines and newspapers. Below is a grid containing two four-letter words; the puzzle is to change the first word into the last word by a series of steps involving the change of just one letter at a time. But at each step the intermediate four letters in each horizontal line must spell a proper word. (The solution will be found at the end of the chapter.)

Is evolution bunk?

L	O	V	E
M	A	L	T

This is not too difficult, but two things have to be noticed. First, the puzzle has been designed to have a solution; the transition would not be possible with just any two four-letter words. Second, the difficulties increase rapidly as we add to the number of letters in the words. Very soon the transition becomes impossible. For example, anyone who can send me a solution to the next puzzle will receive a free, signed copy of this book.

P	U	Z	Z	L	E	R
A	C	H	I	E	V	E

Pathways

Notice here that finding a word that is in some ways intermediate between the two, such as PASSIVE, containing some of the letters from the starting word and some of the letters from the finishing word, is no solution at all. It is the continuous sequence of meaningful words that is of the essence of the puzzle.

This is exactly the problem of finding or imagining links between species, families and orders of living organisms. It may be possible in a very simple case, like that of the species of finches above, to see or imagine such links, but that does not mean it is possible in every case, and indeed in many cases it is manifestly impossible.

Let us take the problem of the bird's lung. One of the characteristics which distinguishes the class of birds is the avian lung. In all other classes of vertebrates, including fish, amphibians, reptiles and mammals, air is drawn into the lungs and expelled through the same passageway, so that the lungs are alternately filled and emptied. In the bird's lung, however, air is moved continuously through the lung, entering and leaving through different passageways.

Of course the bird breathes in and out, but it breathes air into a series of sacs before the lung, like a bagpipe. As the bird breathes out, the sacs of inhaled air are squeezed to produce a continuous flow of air through the lung (or bagpipes). Likewise, in the bird, used air is stored in other sacs the other side of the lung, ready to be expelled when the bird stops breathing in and breathes out.

Is evolution bunk?

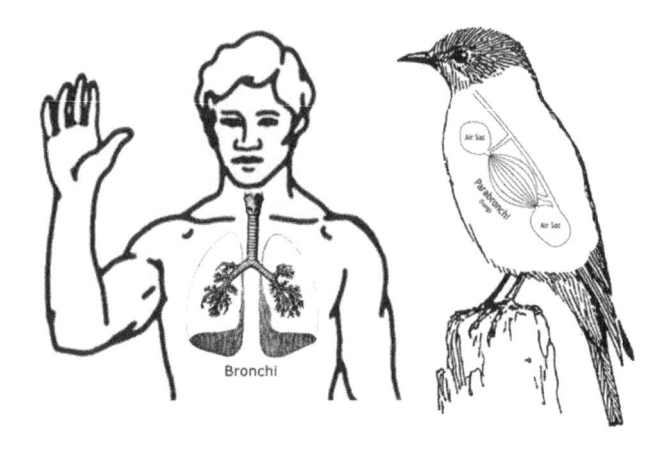

The theory of evolution requires that the bird's respiratory system should have evolved by a series of small changes from the respiratory system of other vertebrates. But the bird's lung is a perfect example of irreducible complexity. To work at all, the system requires a completely different sort of lung, a lung which does not expand and contract like other vertebrate lungs, a lung in which the oxygen is absorbed not in alveoli embedded in the wall of the lung but in a set of parallel parabronchi.

The system also requires special air sacs, more than in the simplified diagram above, for retaining both inhaled air and air to be exhaled, together with all the muscular and nervous systems necessary to control these processes, all of which have no equivalent in other vertebrates. Finally, the system requires a series of pipes connecting these organs to form an essentially circular system, as opposed to the linear vertebrate windpipe.

The first thing to notice is that there are no intermediate forms of lung, either in animals now living, or in the fossil record. Everything has one sort of respiratory system or the other. It is difficult, of course, to imagine what an intermediate form would look like anyway; and that is the point. Notwithstanding that no intermediate forms actually exist or, as far as we know, have ever existed, nevertheless I am prepared to offer another free, signed copy of this book to anyone who can send me a plausible set of drawings showing how one form of lung evolved into the other by a series of small steps, each intermediate step providing a fully functioning breathing apparatus with no spare parts lying around waiting to be used, and in which each change represents some 'evolutionary advantage'.

The bird's lung did not evolve from the lung of the other vertebrates; it had to be designed and made separately, to a different specification, using different principles, different components and a different assembly. As we look at the avian lung we are looking at a special creation.

Compounding the problem of imagining how the avian lung evolved, flight also depends on feathers. More information about feathers will be found in chapter 15, but the problem of the evolution of the feather is just as great as the problem of the evolution of the bird's lung. To cap it all, we have to suppose that the bird's feather and the bird's lung both evolved simultaneously in order to make flight possible – another example of irreducible complexity.

Is evolution bunk?

*** Solution to the puzzle on p. 75. ***

L	O	V	E
M	O	V	E
M	O	L	E
M	A	L	E
M	A	L	T

14

THE PROCESSES OF CHANGE

Darwin observed the small variations in individual members of a species, and proposed that natural selection working on these chance variations had led to the evolution of all living things. In the case of the Galápagos finches he may well have been right, but this mechanism is not able to bridge the much larger gaps in the orders of nature. In 1859 Darwin had no idea of the biochemical structures that underlie inheritance, or how it was that chance produced the variations that he observed. Today, with the invention of the electron microscope and the discovery of DNA, we have a much greater understanding of what is involved than Darwin had. But these advances of modern science have made Darwin's theory not more, but less, plausible.

The characteristics of an organism, from whether it is animal or vegetable to the colour of its skin, all depend on proteins. The recipes for all these proteins are encoded in DNA, with each short section or gene containing the code for a single protein. In the population of a species there is a certain gene pool. For example, in the gene pool of modern human beings, *Homo sapiens*, there are genes which produce blonde hair, brown hair, red hair and black hair. An individual human being carries a different selection of these genes which determine that person's hair colour (apart from the bottle); other individuals carry

Is evolution bunk?

other hair colour genes. When two human beings mate, it is a matter of chance which of their hair colour genes is inherited by their off-spring. It is even possible for a gene to be carried through a generation without any manifest effect, only to reappear in the second generation. This often happens with red hair.

Selection, whether it is natural selection due to environmental factors or human selection due to deliberate inbreeding, involves the preferential selection of some genes and the elimination of others. In dog breeding, a breeder might want to develop a dog with a silky coat. She would then select the animals with silkier coats to breed from, and reject the animals with more wiry coats. In the course of time she could produce a variety with a nice smooth coat that everyone wanted to pat.

She would have done this by eliminating from the line the gene that produces wiry hair. But notice that this process involves a loss of information from the gene pool. The gene pool of the smooth-haired breed no longer contains the gene for wire-haired dogs. If one of the precious smooth-haired pooches escapes while on heat, she may mate with a wire-haired individual and produce a wire-haired mongrel, but the breeder will not be pleased. Within the new breed itself the information for producing wire-haired individuals has been lost.

This explains why islands, like the Galápagos Islands, are notorious for producing extreme variations. The individuals on the island are relatively or completely cut off from the wider gene pool of the species. Any conditions on the island which favour a particular variety of the species will rapidly produce a subspecies which is distinct from the general population on the mainland – larger, smaller, bluer, greener, living up a tree, or living in a hole in the ground. As the subgroup becomes more specialised and genetic information is lost, a new species may evolve,

The processes of change

especially if the same thing is happening in another direction on a neighbouring island. Darwin probably observed the end result of such a process. But in every such case the process involves the loss of genetic information in the gene pool of the subspecies, not the acquisition of new information.

This is true of all processes of selective breeding, whether the selection is done deliberately by people or accidentally by nature. Selection involves a loss of information. But the supposed process of evolution requires the *acquisition* of information at every stage. If indeed the fish gave rise to amphibians, the amphibians to reptiles and the reptiles to birds and mammals, vast quantities of new genetic information had to be added to the DNA at every point. Yet natural selection, as we have seen, contains no mechanism for adding information, only for losing it.

Everything in nature points in the same direction. The Second Law of Thermodynamics, which is universally assumed and observed to be true, states that heat cannot flow from a cold body to a hot body without the input of energy from outside the system. In other words, left to themselves things cool and run down. This is true of everything, from the clock on the mantelpiece to the sun. In theoretical physics this means that, given enough time, the universe itself will run down until everything is uniformly cold and dead; it is called the 'heat death of the universe'.

Put another way, the Second Law of Thermodynamics states that entropy always increases. Entropy is a measure of the state of disorder in a system. Anyone who has ever observed a teenager's bedroom will confirm that disorder always increases. It needs a positive effort on someone's part to preserve or restore order in the system. The general tendency throughout nature is for things to fall

Is evolution bunk?

apart, to disintegrate, to wear out, to die. In biology, the general tendency that we observe is for species to become extinct, for genetic information to be lost. This tendency is now a matter of some ecological concern. The theory of evolution, on the other hand, requires that for long ages this natural tendency was somehow reversed: that genetic information was added, that new species evolved, that entropy decreased, that the chemical elements on Earth became more ordered, that water ran up the hill rather than down.

* * *

There is another mechanism by which change can occur in a species of living organisms. We have looked at the natural variations in the gene pool and seen how selection invariably involves the loss of genetic information. But change can also occur through mutation. Mutation means the random alteration of letters in the genetic code. This may happen through errors being made in the process of copying DNA from one generation to the next.

There are 'proof-reading' devices built in to the system, but occasional errors do occur. Changes may also occur through DNA being exposed to radiation. Such mutations can produce highly abnormal individuals: freaks of nature. But, almost without exception, these freaks are less likely to survive and reproduce than the standard version of the creature. There also appears to be a built-in aversion in every species to such freaks. Freaks are not chosen as mates, so that, even if the individual freak is able to survive and thrive on its own, its faulty genetic make-up is unlikely to be passed on to another generation and to become part of the genetic pool.

The processes of change

If the mutant does interbreed with normal members of the species, there is an in-built tendency for the line to regress to the standard type. As Ariel Roth says, 'Aberrant types tend to be inferior, do not survive in nature, and given a chance, tend to breed back to their original types.'[16] Wherever it has actually been observed, mutation, like selection, is seen to be part of an essentially degenerative process.

The essence of Darwin's theory of evolution is that one species has turned into another by a series of small changes. Darwin himself wrote, 'Natural selection acts solely by accumulating slight, successive, favourable variations; it can produce no great or sudden modifications; it can act only by short and slow steps.' Or, in the motto which has guided generations of evolutionists, 'Nature makes no jumps.' But when we come to consider the processes of selection and mutation in the light of modern knowledge of the biochemical structure of life, we find that there is no genetic mechanism by which evolution can take place.

There is simply no evidence at all that selection can give rise to new information, or that mutation ever leads to anything other than a dead end. Which is, perhaps, the best way to describe the theory of evolution itself: a dead end.

---

[16] Ariel Roth, *Origins*, Review and Herald, 1998, pp. 85–6.

Is evolution bunk?

15

THE FOSSIL RECORD

Fossils are the remains of plants or animals buried in such a way that some or all of their structure when alive has been preserved. They are found extensively in the sedimentary rocks, that is, rocks formed through the deposition of sediment by water, wind or ice. Fossils are found in the sedimentary rocks all over the Earth and under the sea. Unless there has been some sort of upheaval in the sedimentary rocks, it is a logical assumption that the lower strata or layers were laid down before the upper ones. So the sedimentary rocks form some sort of chronological history book.

Generally speaking, it is found that the fossils contained in the lower strata of the rocks are of simpler organisms, like algae, jellyfish, sponges and worms, and that as we work up through the strata we find more and more complex and developed organisms, first marine organisms, then terrestrial ones; first fish, then amphibians, then reptiles, mammals, birds and finally, only in the most recent deposits, *Homo sapiens*. These fossilised remains found in the geologic column are thought to provide one of the most convincing evidences of evolution. But do they?

Actually the fossil record provides convincing evidence against the theory of evolution. The theory of evolution demands that one form of life evolved into another by a

Is evolution bunk?

series of small changes, an essentially gradual process without any sudden jumps. The fossils say the opposite. As each new species appears, it appears fully formed: there are rarely any intermediate stages. Darwin himself realised that the fossil record did not bear out his thesis, but he believed and predicted that as people discovered more fossils, so the gaps would be filled in; people would find 'the missing links'. One hundred and fifty years and millions of fossils later, missing links are still missing.

The fossil record tells a very different story. In the terminology used by modern geologists, the first, abundant multi-celled fossils that bear any resemblance to later forms appear in the Cambrian rocks. There is a clear division between the Precambrian rocks in which very few multi-celled fossils are found and the Cambrian rocks where a great variety of multi-celled fossils are plentiful. The remarkable fact is that in the Cambrian rocks almost all the phyla or main divisions of life appear all at once, without either ancestors or intermediate forms. Palaeontologists call it 'the Cambrian explosion'.

The Cambrian rocks contain the fossils of arthropods or animals with an external skeleton, echinoderms, and chordates or animals with backbones. According to evolutionary theory, this should not be. The phyla should take millions of years to evolve from one another, instead of which many of them appear all at one time. Palaeontologists call the differences between major phyla 'disparity'. The differences within phyla, between classes, orders and families, they call 'diversity'. In the Cambrian rocks, disparity appears before diversity. This is not an evolutionary sequence: the theory of evolution requires that disparity should evolve out of diversity.

In fact the major disparities are there from the beginning. To put the matter more simply: evolution suggests that major differences should grow out of minor differences; in

The fossil record

the fossil record, minor differences grow out of major differences.

Worse than this, the species that first appear in the geologic column are by no means simple. Take, for example, the trilobite. This is one of the commonest of fossils found in the Cambrian rocks. The trilobite was an arthropod with an external skeleton; its body, as its name suggests, was divided into three lobes. But it was not just a shell and a blob of jelly. It had a nervous system and a compound eye.

Simon Ings says, 'The very first trilobite species we know of had eyes. And not blurry, squitty eyes, but gorgeous, faceted, compound eyes, exquisitely constructed and assembled to a design that has never been repeated.'[17] Now, the eye has always been a test for the theory of evolution. Darwin, referring to the human eye, recognised that it was an organ of marvellous complexity and ingenuity; he said himself that 'to suppose that the eye ... could have been formed by natural selection seems, I freely confess, absurd in the highest degree'. There are many different forms of eye in nature, and the eye of the trilobite is a compound eye more like that of a house-fly than a human being. But the compound eye of the trilobite is still a wonderful and sophisticated organ of sight. And yet it appears in the fossil record fully formed, with no sign of evolutionary antecedents.

Then take the evolution of, say, the bat. Evolutionary theory suggests that an original proto-bat (let us call it bat A) evolved from some other small mammal, perhaps a mouse. A small evolutionary change produced a better bat B, which eliminated bat A in the struggle for existence. Then bat C appeared, which eliminated bat B, and so on, until the modern bat Z reached the finishing line. This story

---

[17] Simon Ings, *The Eye, a Natural History*, Bloomsbury 2007.

Is evolution bunk?

accounts for the fact that we only see bat Z in the world today, but we should be able to see something of the evolutionary sequence in the fossil record; there should be at least some fossils of bats A–Y. But that is not the case. The first bat to appear in the fossil record is bat Z, and bat Z remains fundamentally unchanged from then on. In scientific parlance this phenomenon is described as 'sudden appearance followed by stasis'. But that disguises the fact that this is not what the Theory of Evolution requires.

As we look at the animal and vegetable kingdoms today, we see that all living things can be classified according to a series of criteria. We looked briefly at the system that biologists have classically used in a previous chapter. This system has been refined and given a mathematical rigour by the development of the science of cladistics. But, if the theory of evolution is right, such classification should not be possible. There should be a continuous gradation of organisms, at least in the fossil record, showing all the intermediate stages through which the various species have passed in the course of evolution. If we look at the rainbow, we see the seven colours into which it is convenient to divide it: red, orange, yellow, green, blue, indigo, violet. But the colours actually merge into one another in a continuous spectrum; our naming of the colours does not correspond to any radical discontinuities in the rainbow itself. Evolution demands that the same should be true in the world of living things. The phyla, the classes, the orders, the families and the species ought to blend into one another in a seamless progression. In the world as we see it today they do nothing of the sort.

Evolutionists hoped at the beginning that there would emerge just such a seamless progression in the fossil record. But here also there is nothing of the sort. It is true that there are many weird and wonderful creatures now extinct that are buried in the rocks, but most of them are

The fossil record

no more transitional than any of the creatures that we observe today. They too can be assigned according to the same system of phyla, classes, orders, families and species. They are all just as distinct from each other as the animals and plants alive today.

David Quammen, a believer in Darwinism, admits, "The fossil record is like a film of evolution from which 999 out of every 1000 frames have been lost on the cutting room floor."[18] But that is not a film; it is a slide-show, or a series of snap-shots. Put another way: the fossil record is like a chain from which 999 out of every 1000 links is missing. That is simply not a chain. There is no chain of evolution, visible either in the world today or in the fossil record. At best there are short lengths of chain divided from each other by un-bridged, and unbridgeable, gaps.

---

[18] David Quammen, *Was Darwin Wrong?* National Geographic Magazine, November 2004.

Is evolution bunk?

16

HAECKEL'S EMBRYOS

When I was at school, drawings of embryos by the nineteenth-century zoologist Ernst Haeckel helped to persuade me of the truth of the theory of evolution. Haeckel believed with Darwin that all life had evolved by chance from a common source, but he also proposed that in every individual the story of evolution is recapitulated in the womb. He claimed that as the human embryo developed it passed through the different stages of evolution, resembling at one time a fish, then a chicken, then a pig, and only in the latest stage a human being. Haeckel produced drawings of the embryos of all these creatures to demonstrate their similarities.

It is at this point that the image of the white-coated scientist, objectively pursuing the truth, is finally shattered. These drawings were fakes, a deliberate fraud. Worse than that, the fraud was exposed as early as the 1860s, but the drawings continued to be included in biological textbooks; a modified version is still to be found in the well-known encyclopaedia at my side, revised and published in 1993, and the idea of recapitulation is still repeated in television programmes about nature.

The fraud was perpetrated at two levels. First, the drawings were simply inaccurate. Although he had the embryos in front of him, Haeckel drew not what he saw, but what he wanted to see and what he wanted others to

Is evolution bunk?

believe. He deliberately altered the facts to fit the theory. Second, he misrepresented what his drawings showed. He claimed that he had drawn the embryos at an early stage of development. In fact, they were embryos at the mid-stage of development. This is important, because at the early stage of development the embryos are markedly dissimilar; in the earliest stages no one could mistake the embryos for one another. As they develop, the appearance of the embryos converge, before diverging again before birth. The drawings in my own encyclopaedia still claim to be drawings of embryos at an early stage of development, but they are nothing of the sort. The convergence in mid-term is essentially misleading, but has provided the basis for a 'proof' of Darwinism for 150 years.

Sadly, this is not the only example of fraud in the history of the theory of evolution. Probably the most notorious example is Piltdown Man. In 1912 two men claimed to have found a skull, together with extinct animal bones and tools, on Piltdown Common in Sussex, England. The cranium of the skull appeared to be remarkably human, but the jaw was remarkably ape-like. The proximity of the bones of the extinct animals suggested that the skull was of great age, and it was hailed as an early hominid, a missing link between the apes and man. It was 40 years before the fraud was uncovered. When it was, it was proved that the cranium appeared to be remarkably human because it was human, and the jaw appeared to be remarkably ape-like because it was an ape's. The two pieces of the skull were not of the same age, never belonged to the same creature, and the jaw had been heavily doctored to make the apparent match.

Would that this were all ancient history! Much more recently, *National Geographic* magazine announced with a fanfare of trumpets that a fossil had been discovered which appeared to be a missing link between the dinosaurs and the birds. The fossil was named *Archaeoraptor*; it had the

Haeckel's embryos

tail of a dinosaur and the forelimbs of a bird. Here was a feathered dinosaur. This, of course, created a storm of interest, until it was revealed as a fake. A Chinese palaeontologist proved that the back end of a dinosaur had been glued to the front end of a bird. Someone unknown had made what the scientists wanted to find, but in the end, no missing link after all.

In 2005 a professor of anthropology at Frankfurt University was dismissed from his post when it was revealed that he had systematically falsified the dates of relics that he had discovered over a long career. Professor Protsch had identified a fragment of a skull discovered in a Hamburg peat bog as a vital missing link between Neanderthals and modern humans, 36,000 years old. The skull was in fact only 7,500 years old. Another sensational find, 'Binshof-Speyer woman', actually lived in 1300 BC, not 21,300 BC as the professor had claimed; while 'Paderborn-Sande man', whom Protsch had dated at 27,400 BC, had actually died in AD 1750, only a few centuries ago. On his dismissal, a colleague, Professor Terberger, was quoted as saying, 'Anthropology is going to have to completely revise its picture of modern man between 40,000 and 10,000 years ago.'

There is no point in speculating on the motives of the individuals who have perpetrated these frauds: money, professional ambition, desire for fame? This is not to say that all evolutionists are dishonest - of course they are not - but it does go to show that scientists are no more immune to these temptations than anyone else. There are lessons, however, that we should learn from these sorry tales. One is that we should take the announcement of any new 'breakthrough' in the field of evolution with a dose of scepticism.

Scientists working in these fields have shown themselves only too willing to let their imagination run riot with a

Is evolution bunk?

fragment of a thigh and two teeth, and to be gullible subjects for frauds and hoaxes, even when they were not the fraudsters and hoaxers themselves. Particular caution needs to be taken with 'reconstructions' of extinct animals: fragments of fossilised bone or scratchy indentations in the rock can be worked up into drawings and sculptures which owe much more to the artist's imagination than to science.

The media, the newspapers, television and magazines, even some which should know better, are equally gullible or easily deceived. The pattern so often is for a headline to shriek about another discovery that proves our descent from the apes, but when the discovery turns out to be less than momentous, or even fraudulent, there is barely a media squeak. The general public is left with the impression of proof when all that we have, in fact, is another false trail.

Through all these examples runs a single thread: a desperate need to produce evidence for the theory of evolution. At the end of the day, one has to ask oneself, what sort of a theory is it that needs to fake or embroider so much evidence?

17

HOMOLOGY

Another set of drawings which served to convince me as a schoolboy of the case for evolution were those which illustrated the pentadactyl or five-fingered forelimb (see p. 13). These drawings, the reader will be relieved to know, were not fraudulent. They show the forelimbs of a number of vertebrate species, for example bat, bird, man and porpoise. There are indeed remarkable and striking similarities between the structures of these limbs. This is an example of homology. There are many more.

To Darwin, and to many people since, this has seemed to be perhaps the most convincing argument of all for the theory of evolution. Such similarities surely must be due to descent from a common ancestor; each one is a specialised adaptation of the original pattern, one for flight, another for manipulation, another for swimming. All four variations have a single upper bone, the humerus, joined at the elbow to two lower bones, the radius and ulna; these in turn are connected through a number of small knuckly bones, the carpals, to five digits, the first digit being made up of just two small bones, the other four of three or more. This is certainly more than coincidence.

In Darwin's day, the conclusion that these similarities were due to evolution from a common ancestor must have seemed almost irresistible. But further developments in the knowledge of embryology and genetics have now made this conclusion look much less certain.

Is evolution bunk?

Darwin assumed that these limbs developed in the same way in embryo (shades of Haeckel's theory). Today we know that it is nothing like as simple as that. The fact is that many homologous organs develop from entirely different parts of the embryo. Just as the mid-term embryos of various different species may bear a superficial resemblance to one another and yet come from early-term embryos which are radically dissimilar, so organs in various species which end up very similar to one another nevertheless develop from embryonic origins and by embryonic pathways which are entirely dissimilar. For example, a frog's digits grow outwards, whereas human fingers form when the connecting tissue between them undergoes programmed cell death. This is a complete mystery from an evolutionary point of view.

The same is true if we try to relate homology to genes. It is tempting to think that homologous organs, like pentadactyl limbs, are encoded by shared or similar genes. But this does not work either. Geneticists have discovered that apparently homologous structures depend on different genes in different species. Indeed, it appears that there is very rarely a one-to-one correspondence between a gene and a particular characteristic in the organism; one gene can have an input into several different organs, and a similar gene can produce very different results in different species. Despite the progress of genetics in the last twenty years the study of how the body arranges the proteins derived from its DNA into different organs is far from understood. Much is still a mystery. But it is clear that there is no simple explanation for the observed facts of homology in either embryology or genetics.

The Darwinian explanation of homology went like this: we observe that a number of travellers have arrived at hotels in the same city, the city being the modern era; their accommodation varies from a five-star penthouse suite for honeymoon couples to the local youth hostel. But each

Homology

visitor has the same basic facilities: a bed, a table, a chair and a shower, and they are all staying in the same city – they are homologous. Therefore, the Darwinian argument goes, they must all have started out from the same place; they must have come by the same route; and their paths only diverged at the end when they headed for their own specialised accommodation.

The fallacy is obvious. In fact, as embryology and genetics have now demonstrated, our homologous travellers often start out from different places and travel by different routes. The fact that their arrangements converge at the end of their journey is only due to the fact that they all have the same basic needs. The evolutionists even have their own version of this process: it is called convergent evolution, but it is the opposite of the classical argument for evolution from homology.

A better explanation of homology lies in design. Consider wheels. A wheel is a human design; animals, and even human beings, do not run on wheels.

Is evolution bunk?

Wheels crop up in many different forms: a bicycle has wheels; the London Eye is a wheel; there are wheels in the movement of my wristwatch (an old-fashioned one that I have had for over 50 years); a cart and a steam train have wheels. Does this mean that a bicycle, the London Eye, a wristwatch, a cart and a steam train are all in some way derived from a common ancestor? No, it just means that the wheel is a very versatile and efficient piece of design technology which generations of intelligent designers have adapted to different uses.

Once we have embraced the idea of intelligent design, and therefore of a Designer, the mystery of homology becomes clear. Homology is due not to evolution, but to a piece of brilliant design that can be adapted and applied to a variety of situations: to the bat's and the bird's wing, to the human arm, and to the porpoise's flipper. More than this, the fact that homologous organs are actually formed by such different embryological pathways and depend on such different genes means that each kind of animal, however homologous its organs, is a special creation.

18

A VERDICT ON THE EVIDENCE

We have been looking at some of the principal pieces of evidence which evolutionists have brought forward to support their theory. It is time to consider our verdict on this evidence, and to ask whether another theory, the theory of creation, does not fit the facts better.

We have examined four areas of enquiry:

1. The variation in the peppered moth brought about by industrialisation.
2. The fossil record.
3. Haeckel's drawings of embryos.
4. The phenomenon of homology illustrated in the five-fingered limb.

Let us once again ask how our two theories deal with these issues, starting with the *theory of evolution*.

1. There is no argument that variation occurs in nature, or that in certain circumstances natural selection causes one variant to become dominant. The question is, how far can changes due to this mechanism go. Evolution demands that such change be limitless, but there are very strong arguments that this is not so. First, major changes have

Is evolution bunk?

never been observed in nature or in selective breeding by humans; cats have never been bred from dogs. Scientists have experimented extensively on breeding fruit-flies and have produced many strange mutations, but they have never produced anything other than strange fruit-flies.

In lieu of any experimental or observational evidence for macro-evolution, evolutionists must be able to propose theoretical pathways by which major changes in organisms might have occurred. However, when we begin to consider what is involved in the construction, for example, of the avian lung or feather, we come up once more against the problem of irreducible complexity, and we find that there are apparently insurmountable barriers to macro-evolution. Moreover, selection leads invariably to the loss of genetic information, but evolution requires the addition of genetic information. Evolution is unable to suggest any mechanism for the increase of information in the evolutionary process. On the contrary, every other process in nature shows the opposite tendency: the increase of entropy.

2. The fossil record, contained in the sedimentary rocks, does indeed show a rough and ready progression from the simplest organisms to the more advanced. This is a fact that does require an explanation, since it is not self-explanatory. At first sight evolution appears a plausible theory. But there are fatal flaws in the fossil record.

The first is the lack of the necessary missing links. The fossils rarely show a seamless transition from one major group of organisms to another in any steady evolutionary series. On the contrary, they show that each type of organism, as soon as it appears, appears fully formed and remarkably distinct from all other organisms. Complicated organs, like the eye, do not appear in the fossil record gradually; when the trilobite eye appears, it appears

A verdict on the evidence

already complete. Second, the fossil succession is not as clearly evolutionary as it might seem at first. Referring to work done by fossil expert Kurt Wise, Paul Garner writes, 'When the actual order of first appearance of the major fossil groups (kingdoms, phyla, classes) is compared with the order in which they ought to have appeared, there seems to be little correspondence. Out of 144 test cases, only 5 showed a significant agreement between the fossil order and the predicted evolutionary order.'[19]

3. Haeckel's embryos introduced us to the sorry story of, at best, overexcited imagination and, at worst, fraud in the theory of evolution. But Haeckel had a point, even though he spoiled his case by overstating or overdrawing it. At mid-term there is a striking resemblance between the embryos of many creatures. It is indeed tempting to seek an explanation for this in evolution. But further examination reveals these similarities to be misleading. The early embryos from which they come, and the later embryos into which they develop, simply do not show the required degree of similarity.

4. It is the same story with homology. The similarities in the pentadactyl limbs of many vertebrates almost forces us to believe that they have a common ancestor, until we examine more closely how these limbs are actually formed in the different species. To our surprise we find that they are actually formed from different parts of the embryo, and depend on different genes in the DNA. The end product may look remarkably similar, but the process of manufacture in each case is very different. This

---

[19] Paul Garner, *The New Creationism*, Evangelical Press 2009, p.197. This book gives an excellent resumé of the latest Creationist research.

Is evolution bunk?

undermines the evolutionary theory of their relationship and forces us to look elsewhere for an explanation.

Homology is a fact, whether at the level of the similarities of pentadactyl limbs or at the level of similarities of DNA – humans share 96% of their DNA with chimpanzees, and even share 46% of their DNA with bananas. But homology can be misleading. We saw earlier in the book how there are many homologous features between a motor-car and a horse-drawn carriage: wheels, seats, doors and windows, even lamps. But it would be misleading to suppose that therefore one is simply the evolutionary descendant of the other. The motor-car may have come after the horse-drawn carriage, and it may perform a similar function, but the horse did not turn into an internal combustion engine. The internal combustion engine was a new and special creation of intelligent human design.

The differences between the horse-drawn carriage and the motor-car, such as the method of propulsion, are as important or more important than the similarities. In the same way, the differences between humans and chimpanzees are much greater than the 4% difference in their DNA. Chimpanzees have not written 96% of the works of Shakespeare, or 96% of the music of Mozart, and bananas have not written any at all.

Always there are two possible explanations of homology: one is indeed common ancestry, as the evolutionists suggest. This explanation supposes that because we share 96% of our DNA with the chimps and 46% with bananas, human beings therefore share a common ancestor with the chimpanzees and even with bananas. But the argument is doubtful, if not absurd.

Once we have embraced the idea of design in nature, we have a much more plausible explanation for homology: an intelligent Designer has taken the basic chemicals of the

A verdict on the evidence

universe and made them into different things, a human being, a chimpanzee and a banana. If one piece of design pops up with many different applications, like the wheel, it simply means that the wheel is a very adaptable piece of design technology.

We find, then, that none of the evidence brought forward by the evolutionists stands up to cross-examination. In some cases, like the fossil record, the evidence sometimes suggests the exact opposite of what it was called upon to do; in other cases, it turns out to have other explanations. So how does the *theory of creation* deal with the facts?

According to this theory, all living things, animal and vegetable, were created in the beginning by God: bananas, chimpanzees and human beings, each according to its kind. It was God who designed and created the amazing microworld of the cell; God who wrote the information for each living creature in its DNA; God who built variation between individuals into his creation. Each kind of plant and animal is a special creation, both designed and made in its perfect form. Each species is capable of a measure of adaptation to its particular circumstances, so that, for example, human skin can be black in very hot, sunny climates and white in colder, darker latitudes, the beaks of finches are adaptable to the food supply on each island where they live; and, from the Pekinese to the Great Dane, the range of possible adaptations can be remarkably large. Exactly how far variation within species and even separate speciation can go before the process meets insuperable obstacles is an unresolved question. But many of the organs which we have studied, like the bird's lung and feather, or the human and the trilobite eye, are not adaptations of anything else, but are special creations.

The masterful ingenuity and cunning that is displayed at every point in the anatomy and biochemistry of every living creature is precisely what it seems: the result of

Is evolution bunk?

intelligent design and the work of an intelligent Designer. Truly the seraphim are not exaggerating when they say, 'The whole earth is full of his glory.'

There are, however, unanswered questions about the rocks, and to these we must turn next.

19

THE SEDIMENTARY ROCKS

There are some basic questions about the sedimentary rocks which we need to answer, such as: how old are they, and how were they laid down? The sedimentary rocks are the fossil-bearing rocks, so the history of the sedimentary rocks is inextricably linked with the history of the fossils, and because the fossils are an important part of the theory of evolution, the history of the sedimentary rocks is also inextricably linked to the theory of evolution.

In 1830 Charles Lyell published a book about the *Principles of Geology*. Building on the ideas of the eighteenth-century geologist James Hutton, Lyell proposed what came to be called the principle of uniformity. This states that 'the present is the key to the past'. In other words, the geological processes and conditions that we see in the world today have always remained the same and explain the geological past: geological processes and conditions have always been uniform. In terms of the formation of sedimentary rocks, the main geological processes concerned are weathering, erosion and deposition or sedimentation.

If you look at the statues on the façade of a medieval cathedral you see that the features of the figures are often worn away; this is the geological process of weathering. A footpath in the English Lake District, if overused by walkers, becomes a gully in which the soil is progressively

Is evolution bunk?

washed away by the rain; this is the process of erosion. A river in spate after heavy rain is thick with mud, and if the storm has been particularly violent, the river often carries branches, even whole trees, and other debris along. When the water becomes calmer, the solid matter suspended in the turbulent water settles out and is deposited again; this is the geological process of sedimentation. The principle of uniformity asserts that it is these same processes, operating at similar rates to those that we observe today, which account for the formation of the sedimentary rocks.

Three objections to this idea immediately suggest themselves. The first concerns the sites of deposition. Sedimentation occurs today on the flood plains of rivers, in lakes, in deltas, on the seashore, and where rivers disgorge their burden of sediment further out to sea. But how many of these features occur near you? Or how many such sedimentation sites could you find within 100 miles of where you live? Yet three quarters of the earth's surface is covered by sedimentary rocks. The Jurassic Morrison Formation in the western USA, which contains many dinosaur fossils, covers over one million square kilometres from Canada to Texas. Nowhere in the world today is sedimentation occurring on this scale, and indeed it is difficult to imagine any of the processes that we observe today being responsible for such huge areas of sedimentary rock.

Second, sedimentary rocks are sometimes extremely thick. The Old Red Sandstone, which covers half of Scotland and contains many fish fossils, is over 2,700 metres (9,000 feet) thick, more than twice the height of the highest mountain in Scotland, Ben Nevis. Moreover, there are signs, as we shall see later, that these deposits were laid down very quickly. There is no process occurring on Earth today which can account for these rocks.

The sedimentary rocks

Third, sedimentation results in relatively even, horizontal layers. But this is not the form in which most of the sedimentary rocks are found today: they are bent, folded, sometimes even folded double – 'as if they were made of putty' as one geology textbook describes them; they are tilted up at every angle, sometimes vertically; they are intruded by and even overlaid with great masses of non-sedimentary rock. In many places the sedimentary rocks, which must have been formed underwater, have been uplifted to enormous heights at the top of mountain ranges like the Himalayas and the Rockies. Large amounts of igneous rock, produced by volcanic eruption or intrusion, are now found below, between and above the layers of sedimentary rock. Like the sedimentary rocks, these igneous rocks sometimes cover vast areas: the Columbia Plateau in North America is a stack of lava sheets covering 500,000 square kilometres (200,000 square miles) and sometimes hundreds of metres thick. All this indicates that volcanic activity once took place on a scale that is unknown today.

Geologists ascribe these phenomena, folding, uplifting, intrusion and volcanism, to the movement of the Earth's tectonic plates. These movements account for the earthquakes, tsunamis and volcanic eruptions that occur from time to time today. With modern satellite technology it is indeed possible to measure such tectonic movements, showing, for example, that America is moving away from Europe at the rate of about 2 centimetres per year. But it is difficult to believe that the level of seismic, volcanic and tectonic activity that we see today could be responsible for the dramatic deformations and upheavals of the past; the rocks speak of a past that was much more violent and turbulent than the present.

The geological processes at work today, of weathering, erosion and sedimentation, or of mountain building and continental drift, are extremely slow, almost

Is evolution bunk?

imperceptible. Over, say, 1,000 years it is possible to see differences in the landscape, but even then the differences are small. In eastern England, there are villages like Cley-next-the-Sea which were once thriving ports but which lost all their trade and declined as their rivers silted up. On the other hand, in the Middle Ages the town of Dunwich was one of the most important in East Anglia, until the waves ate the cliffs and the buildings one by one tumbled into the sea.

Yet these are only minor alterations in the coastline when we look at the region as a whole. Proponents of the principle of uniformity have always been aware that so gradual are the geological processes operating today that vast ages of time would be necessary if they were to explain the formation of the rocks and the landscape that we now see. Not just thousands, but millions and even billions of years, so-called geological time, has to be supposed to maintain the principle of uniformity.

But now we are beginning to see the parallels between the geological principle of uniformity and the theory of evolution. The small changes that we observe in the world around us are extrapolated into large, unobservable changes by the intervention of extraordinary ages of time. Micro-evolution is supposed to become macro-evolution given enough time. Micro-sedimentation is supposed to become mega-sedimentation given enough time. So enough time is invented and, behold, everyone can believe in the principle of uniformity and the theory of evolution. Except that a lot of the evidence contradicts both. Lyell and Darwin made the same mistake, and for the same reason. The principle of uniformity and the theory of evolution are like husband and wife. Lyell and Darwin became parents-in-law: their theories formed an indissoluble union. Just as the fossils are embedded in the rocks, so the theory of evolution is embedded in the principle of uniformity.

The sedimentary rocks

But never in the history of science has such a completely arbitrary idea as the principle of uniformity so quickly become a scientific dogma in the face of so much evidence to the contrary. So overwhelming is the evidence against it that even evolutionists are now admitting that there must be exceptions to the principle of uniformity. Catastrophism is back on the geologists' agenda.

Is evolution bunk?

20

CATASTROPHE

In the last 40 years geologists have begun to re-examine the role of catastrophe in the history of the Earth. Leonard Brand writes in *Geoscience Reports*, 'The science of geology has abandoned Charles Lyell's rigid uniformitarianism, and is recognizing the important role of catastrophe in Earth history.'[20] The strongest evidence that the Earth has a catastrophic past comes, ironically, from the very fossils themselves. In today's conditions fossilisation is a rare event. It is supposed to occur when a living organism, whether it is a leaf or a tree, a fish or a rabbit, dies and falls to the ground. Where it falls, either onto dry land or into water, it is slowly buried in wind- or water-borne sediment. But this rarely happens, because, as soon as the organism dies, the natural processes of decomposition set in, animals and birds scavenge, maggots and insects feed on the decaying body, and soon all is dust. If the present is the key to the past, there should not be many fossils at all, and those that exist should not resemble the ones we actually find in the ground.

In north-eastern Brazil there are extensive fossil-bearing rocks known as the Santana Formation. They contain some of the best-preserved fossils in the world. There are many fish, as well as reptiles such as turtles, crocodiles and

---

[20] Leonard Brand, 'Catastrophes and Earth History', *Geoscience Reports*, Winter 1994.

Is evolution bunk?

dinosaurs, and insects such as dragonflies and beetles. But the fish are the most remarkable specimens. All the evidence suggests that they were buried extremely rapidly, before any sort of decomposition could begin; palaeontologists estimate that they were killed and buried within an hour. Most of the fish still have their scales intact, some of the fossils maintain their three-dimensional form, with soft tissues and even eyeballs petrified but still as they were at the moment of death. When a fish dies, one of the first indications of decay is the loss of scales. The full array of scales on these fossil fish is a strong indication of the extreme rapidity of their burial and preservation.

With this in view, let us return to the Old Red Sandstone that covers half of Scotland. As well as vast quantities of stones and boulders, there are embedded in these rocks the fossils of hundreds of thousands of fish. These fish did not die a natural death, nor did they sink to the bottom to be buried by the tranquil deposition of sediment. To quote Hugh Miller, who investigated these rocks in the nineteenth century,

> The remains exhibit unequivocal marks of violent death. The figures are contorted, contracted, curved; the tail in many instances is bent round to the head; the spines stick out, the fins are spread to the full, as in fish that die in convulsions. The attitudes of all the fish fossils are attitudes of fear, anger and pain. The remains, too, appear to have suffered nothing from the after-attacks of predaceous fishes; none such seem to have survived. The record is one of destruction, at once widespread and total.[21]

---

[21] Hugh Miller, *The Old Red Sandstone*, J. Johnstone, 1841, p.222.

Catastrophe

Fish swim in the sea; water is their natural habitat. The fish of the Santana Formation and of the Old Red Sandstone have been overwhelmed in very large numbers by some sudden catastrophe, killing and burying them very quickly. Amongst the fossilised fish there are several which have been caught half way through their dinner: fish fossilized with a smaller fish half way down the throat, predator and prey fossilised together in mid-swallow. Whatever happened to these fish was a catastrophe, 'widespread and total'.

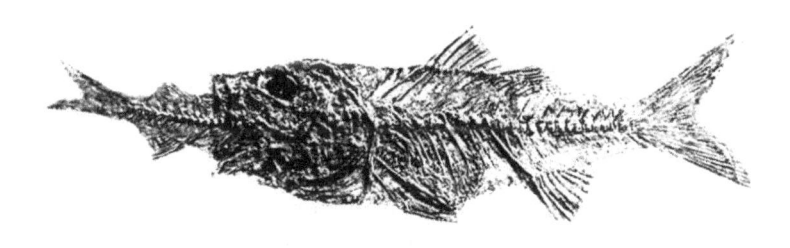

In the Grand Canyon in Arizona, there is a formation of rock known as the Redwall Limestone. Uniformitarian geology would reckon that such a limestone would be deposited at the rate of about 30 centimetres (1 foot) per 1,000 years. However, the Redwall Limestone has recently been discovered to contain billions of nautiloids, squid-like marine animals with a hard, straight shell sometimes 60 centimetres (2 feet) long. By the way that they lie, it is plain that these fossil nautiloids have been buried instantaneously in a fast-moving underwater slurry. These rocks have not been deposited over thousands of years, but in hours, if not minutes.

Is evolution bunk?

The permafrost of Siberia, in particular on the Liakhov Islands of northern Siberia, contains other astonishing animal graveyards. Thousands of woolly mammoths are frozen in the ground, as if in some gigantic deep-freeze. Some are found complete with flesh, skin and hair, and even with undigested food in their stomachs. When they are dug up, as they are for their ivory tusks, their thawed flesh is sometimes still edible for wolves and sledge-dogs. Perhaps, more astonishing still, they are found alongside woolly rhinoceros, musk ox, saiga antelope, reindeer, tiger, arctic fox, bear and horse, creatures which require forest, meadow and steppe as habitat, rather than the frozen wastes of Siberia. These creatures did not die in their beds, nor were they eaten by predators. They were overtaken by a sudden catastrophe.

We do not even have to go to Siberia to find such graveyards; they are all over the world. In some, such as at Geiseltal in Germany, vertebrate animals, insects and plants are found compressed together, still showing details of hair, feathers and scales, stomach contents and even crocodile's pooh. In others, such as the bone-beds at Agate Springs in Nebraska, thousands of bones have been found jumbled together, from animals as varied as rhinoceros, camel and giant boar. In the Baltic amber deposits were discovered the fossilised parts of insects and flowers from every region on Earth. These fossil graveyards are not the result of any event that we see currently taking place on Earth; the present is no explanation of the past. This is the result of a catastrophe or catastrophes, comparable to nothing in the world today.

The evidence is no less compelling when we turn to the evidence of fossilised plants. In many parts of the world, fossilised tree trunks can be found in an upright position, standing through several successive layers of sedimentary rock. According to the principle of uniformity, these fossilised trees are inexplicable. The rock strata should

Catastrophe

have taken thousands of years to form, at some stages the tree trunks standing in water, at others on dry land, as the sediment crept up, then stopped, then crept up again. Dead wood rots and is eaten by insects and grubs in just a few years. Few trees die on their feet in any case; most die as a result of being blown over. It is clear that several layers of sedimentary rock were deposited around these upright trunks very quickly. The present is not the key to the past.

Coal is equally mysterious. Coal is formed from vegetable matter, from trees and plants, which is collected together in deep layers and then compressed by the weight of rocks above. Uniformitarian geology suggests that this sort of accumulation of dead vegetable matter might have taken place in swamps and peat bogs, such as the Dismal Swamp in Virginia. But, again, how many swamps and peat bogs are there near you? Yet the world contains vast coal deposits spread over every continent, even Antarctica.

The Dismal Swamp in Virginia has accumulated about 2.5 metres (8 feet) of peat, which compressed into coal would form a seam a few centimetres thick. But there are coal seams in the world 9–12 metres (30–40 feet) in thickness, which would have required plant remains 90–120 metres (300–400 feet) deep. Then there are places where there are up to 75 separate seams of coal, one on top of the other, separated by layers of other sedimentary rock. Moreover, much of the vegetation is the Carboniferous coal layers appears to be aquatic, suggesting that the plants are not terrestrial ones at all, but that it originated in a vast 'floating forest.' What we need in order to explain coal are not a few little peat bogs, but a giant catastrophe which stripped large areas of the earth and sea of all green things, deposited the debris in deep beds, and buried them under tons of sediment, over and over again.

Something which has long puzzled palaeontologists studying the fossil record has been the extinction of the

Is evolution bunk?

dinosaurs. According to their own geological timescale, the dinosaurs died out about 65 million years ago, at least relatively suddenly. The favourite explanation at the moment is a disruption of the Earth's climate caused by the impact of a giant meteorite. This, at least, is not uniformitarianism; it is the invocation of catastrophism, of one sort or another. But another feature of the story of the dinosaurs also requires explanation: dinosaur graveyards.

The Morrison Formation in Utah and Colorado contains a mass of bones representing over 300 species of dinosaur, as well as snails and mammals. But the bones are not scattered about evenly over the area covered by the rock formation; they are collected together in huge fossilised heaps. They have been transported to their final resting place by water. Whatever catastrophe killed these dinosaurs, it killed them all at once and collected their bones together.

So we are looking for some worldwide catastrophe or series of catastrophes which killed fish and marine organisms, animals, insects, plants and dinosaurs in incredible numbers; a catastrophe which struck suddenly, not only causing widespread death and destruction, but collecting together in heaps various types of organism, burying them and petrifying them in sedimentary rock; a catastrophe which also involved widespread volcanism, upheavals in the Earth's crust and the movement or creation of the world's continents.

21

THE FLOOD

If we are looking for any worldwide catastrophe, it is sheer perversity to discount the one which is remembered by the whole human race and of which there are accounts in the historical record: the Flood. The well-known anthropologist Sir James Frazer collected over 100 traditions of a universal Flood in the folklore of peoples from every continent on Earth: Europe, Asia, Australia, the East Indies, Melanesia, Micronesia, Polynesia, South America, North America and East Africa. Over 500 such stories are now known. There are written accounts of the Flood in the literature of the ancient Sumerians, Babylonians (*The Epic of Gilgamesh*) and the Jews. There are significant differences in these stories, but also significant similarities. Just because the story of Noah's Ark is to be found on the bookshelf of almost every child in the Western world, it is sheer prejudice to reject it as the answer to our question.

The story of the Flood in the ancient literature of the Jews is to be found in the book of Genesis, from chapter 6:9 to chapter 9:19 (the division of the Bible into chapters and verses is a modern invention). In addition there are verses in the Psalms, ancient Jewish hymns in praise of God, which could also be descriptive of the same event, e.g. Psalm 104:5–9. This literature is what we might call pre-scientific; it does not describe the Flood in the sort of terms

Is evolution bunk?

that geologists use today. Indeed, the writers have a different focus altogether, a focus on God and what we would call the human interest. Nevertheless, it is perfectly possible to see the geological and palaeontological outlines of what is being described. We will list the points (some modern translations of the Bible will make these points clearer than others; quotations here are taken from the Revised Standard Version, unless otherwise indicated).

- 'The earth was filled with violence' (Genesis 6:11). This sounds a fair description of the age of the dinosaurs, judging by what we know of them. It is clear from verses 12, 13 and 17 that the corruption and violence are endemic not only in human beings, but in all living creatures.
- 'In the six hundredth year of Noah's life, in the second month, on the seventeenth day of the month. . .' (Genesis 7:11). By comparing this verse with 8:13–14 we see that the flood event lasted over a year in all.
- 'On that day all the fountains of the great deep burst forth, and the windows of the heavens were opened' (Genesis 7:11). The 40 days and nights of rain are what feature in all the children's story-books, but the Bible makes it clear that the waters of the Flood came from below the earth as much as from above. In the stories of creation earlier in Genesis, it is said that God 'separated the waters which were under the firmament [sky] from the waters which were above the firmament' (Genesis 1:7). There is still a lot of water trapped in the Earth's crust. The implication is that before the Flood there was a great deal more, and that the Flood involved not just a lot of rain, but the sudden and catastrophic release of vast quantities of water from under the earth also. This itself cannot have taken place without massive convulsions in the Earth's crust,

The Flood

convulsions which must have been associated with extensive volcanic eruptions.
- 'The waters prevailed so mightily upon the earth that all the high mountains under the whole heaven were covered . . . fifteen cubits [7 metres] deep' (Genesis 7:19). We do not know how high the pre-Flood mountains were, but we have to imagine all the waters of our present oceans churning all over the Earth, pulled back and forth by the tides, alternately coming to rest and depositing their colossal burdens of mud, sand, silt and debris, both animal and vegetable, and then plunging on in fresh torrents. Nothing better or more completely accounts for the entombment of fossils in sediment, the folding, fracturing and overthrusting of the rocks, the fossil graveyards, the coal beds and the sheets of lava that form the surface of the Earth as we see it today.
- 'He blotted out every living thing that was upon the face of the ground' (Genesis 7:23). The fossil record shows that many of the fish and marine organisms also perished in this inundation, but so did all the land-dwelling creatures, except those that were with Noah in the Ark. The waters transported their bodies and bones from all over the world to their final resting places, as the waters receded. If an explanation is to be sought for the rough sequence in which the different classes of animals are found in the fossil record, it lies not in the sequence of their evolution, but in their relative location in the ecology of the Earth before the Flood, and in their behaviour and mobility during the Flood.
- 'The fountains of the deep and the windows of the heavens were closed, the rain from the heavens was restrained, and the waters receded from the earth continually' (Genesis 8:2–3).

Is evolution bunk?

- Other Scriptures also preserve some memory or tradition of the Flood, which help to fill in the gaps in our understanding:

    The Lord, the LORD Almighty,
    he who touches the earth and it melts,
    and all who live in it mourn –
    the whole land rises like the Nile,
    then sinks like the river of Egypt –
    he who builds his lofty palace in the heavens
    and sets its foundation on the earth,
    who calls for the waters of the sea
    and pours them out over the face of the land –
    the LORD is his name. (Amos 9:5–6, NIV)

    And from Psalm 104:6–9:

    Thou didst cover it [the earth] with the deep as with a garment; the waters stood above the mountains.
    At thy rebuke they fled; at the sound of thy thunder they took to flight.
    The mountains rose, the valleys sank down to the place which thou didst appoint for them.
    Thou didst set a bound which they should not pass, so that they might not again cover the earth.
    (RSV, which preserves the literal Hebrew meaning)

This is the description that we need, not just of the Flood itself, but of the 'melting' of the crust of the Earth, of mountain building, of the formation of the deep-sea basins and trenches, of Earth's valleys and canyons. This must have involved serious movements in the Earth's tectonic plates, during and after the year of the Flood, causing yet more volcanism and the twisting, folding, uplifting and

The Flood

sculpting of the newly formed rocks at the time when they were indeed 'made of putty'.

The Flood explains many of the geological facts which are inexplicable from a uniformitarian point of view: first, the rapid burial in water-borne sediments of so many animals, including fish, to which the fossil record bears witness; second, the accumulation of fossils in 'graveyards' like the Morrison Formation; third, the vast sheets of marine sediments that cover all the continents; fourth, the lack of either physical or chemical erosion between the layers of sedimentary rocks, which indicate that they were laid down rapidly, one after the other; and fifth, the large-scale folding, faulting and overthrusting of the rocks when they were in a relatively plastic state. In addition it is most unlikely that, after such a massive disruption of the geology of the Earth, the planet would settle down to a new equilibrium immediately. After the Flood, there would probably have been continued volcanism and movement of the Earth's crust, leading to further local catastrophes in the years that followed.

There are many questions of detail which geologists could and should continue to investigate about the Flood as an alternative to the principle of uniformity. At the present time there are by no means answers to all these questions. As long ago as 1961 Whitcomb and Morris presented, in a book called *The Genesis Flood*, an outline of a Flood geology which, while it might have to be modified in the light of more recent research, provides a structure for further enquiry. Meanwhile, the theory of Noah's Flood is altogether a simpler and better explanation of the outstanding features of the landscape than the principle of uniformity or any alternative catastrophe that we might invent, and the Flood is a catastrophe attested by peoples all over the Earth.

Is evolution bunk?

22

MOUNT ST HELENS

On the 18th May 1980 one of the most devastating volcanic eruptions of modern times took place in Washington State, USA. Mount St Helens exploded with the force of 30,000 atomic bombs. The eruption blew out the entire north face of the mountain, lowering its summit by more than 400 metres (1,200 feet). The initial blast flattened over 500 square kilometres (200 square miles) of forest, stripping the trees of foliage and branches and snapping off or uprooting the trunks. Pyroclastic flows of ash and pumice, and torrents of mud, raced down the mountain and its surrounding valleys, as a mushroom cloud of ash rose over 18 kilometres (11 miles) into the sky.

The initial eruption lasted for nine hours, but the mountain went on erupting, spewing forth more ash and pumice and causing more mud flows, for the rest of 1980 and on through the next five years. Activity did not finally stop until the 2000s, when Mount St Helens fell silent again for the time being. As a result of the 1980 eruption and its aftermath not only the mountain itself, but also the surrounding countryside, especially the North Fork of the Toutle River valley and the nearby Spirit Lake, were radically impacted.

The significance of this volcanic eruption is that it happened at a time and in a place where scientists were able to make unique observations of the event itself and its

Is evolution bunk?

longer- term consequences. This was a real-life geological catastrophe, taking place before our very eyes. Many of the observations that the scientists made shed extraordinary light on the processes that have been the object of our study in the last few chapters.

As we have seen, uniformitarian geology suggests that the strata of sedimentary rock took many thousands or even millions of years to lay down, each change in the strata representing a change in the climate and environment in which it was laid down. Canyons and gorges, like the Grand Canyon in Arizona, and the Tarn and Verdon gorges in France, are amongst the most spectacular features of the present-day landscape, cutting through and exposing these beds of sedimentary rock, where they lie one on top of the other. Uniformitarian geology again suggests that these canyons took millions of years to form – for example, the Grand Canyon was said to have been eroded by the Colorado River which now flows at its base. So we have millions of years for the sedimentary rocks to form and then millions of years more while they are eroded away to form the canyons and gorges that we see today.

However, in the valley of the North Fork of the Toutle River today there are canyons which were formed in a matter of months: Step Canyon is up to 215 metres (700 feet) deep and Loowit Canyon up to 30 metres (100 feet) deep. One cliff, formed by pyroclastic flows and mud flows from the volcano, cutting through the debris of previous eruptions, displays three distinct layers: the bottom third represents the layer of ash deposited by the initial eruption on the 18th May 1980; the middle third, some 7.5 metres (25 feet) deep, containing many thin layers or beds, was deposited on another day, the 12th June 1980; the top layer resulted from a mud flow on the 19th March 1982. The rocks in this 'mini-Grand Canyon' did not take millions of years to lay down, but less than two years; it did not take

Mount St Helens

millions of years to erode this canyon, but a single day. The little stream of the Toutle River that now flows through the valley at the base of the canyon is not the cause of the canyon, but the result of the canyon. The canyon is not there because of the river; the river is there because of the canyon. Thus we see landscape features, which had been supposed to represent long ages in the past, being formed in the geological blink of an eye.

By modern standards the eruption of Mount St Helens was a major geological event, but in terms of the surface of the whole Earth it was the popping of a pimple on an elephant. But it does enable us to see the processes that could have been at work during the Flood, laying down vast sheets both of lava and of sedimentary rock in a single year, and eroding great canyons through the recently formed rock in days. It is another geological story altogether, but one which we have now seen re-enacted before our own eyes.

The upright fossil trees which have been found, extending through several layers of sedimentary rock, have always puzzled uniformitarian geologists. Light has also been shed on this mystery by the eruption of Mount St Helens. One of the puzzling features of these petrified forests has been that the trees lacked branches, but still retained a root ball. However, after the Mount St Helens eruption many trees were found in Spirit Lake in exactly this condition. Their branches and foliage had been stripped by the blast and they had been torn from the ground, leaving a bare trunk and a root ball. Washed or blasted into the lake, they either floated in an upright position, or in some cases sank down and stood upright on the bottom due to the weight of the root ball. Only five years after the initial blast, divers found that already the trees at the bottom of the lake were being trapped in sediments which were being deposited around them.

Is evolution bunk?

Meanwhile the foliage, the smaller branches and the bark from millions of trees devastated by the volcano also collected at the bottom of Spirit Lake, forming a peat bed. If this peat, laid down, not in a dismal swamp over thousands of years, but in a day, were to be buried again under fresh layers of lava or sedimentary rock, the heat and pressure of the rock above would quickly convert it into coal.

The eruption of Mount St Helens and the train of events which it set in motion have done much to confirm the speculation that the geological formation of the Earth is the result not of slow uniformitarian processes, but of a sudden and worldwide catastrophe. It has shown that the landscape can be rearranged in a matter of hours, that the deposition of sedimentary rocks and the erosion of canyons can take place in days, and that coal can be formed in years. Millions or billions of years are not required: the Flood could do the job in the twinkling of an eye. If we abandon the theory of evolution, we do not need the millions of years required for the species to evolve by random mutation. What Darwin could only do in billions of years, God could do in a matter of days. If we abandon the theory of uniformity, we do not need the millions of years required for the formation of the rocks and the fossils. What Lyell could only do in billions of years, the Flood could do in one. At the click of a mouse, we can delete billions of years of the Earth's supposed history, and we are left with an Earth possibly only a few thousand years old. Is that possible? Let us see.

23

THE YOUNG EARTH: 1

Try to forget that you ever heard that the Earth was millions of years old, and simply look at the world around you. The long ages were required by uniformitarians to allow time for the rocks to form, and by evolutionists to allow time for the species to evolve. But there are other clues to the real age of the Earth to be found in the world around us.

Start with trees. Trees are the oldest living organisms on earth. Some conifers seem to be virtually everlasting. Trees like the California Redwood and the Bristlecone Pine do not seem to go through an aging process like deciduous trees, and they seem to be immune from disease. Trees also keep a record of their birthdays, unlike most creatures, in the form of tree-rings. So we know how old the oldest trees are: somewhat over 4,000 years. Since these trees seem to be capable of going on for ever, we have to ask, why are there no trees older than this? The answer could be that all trees were destroyed by the Flood. The trees that we see today are the first growth after the Flood, grown from cones and seeds deposited in the muds and silts left by the receding waters.

Next, let us visit Niagara Falls. These waterfalls lie on the border between the USA and Canada and are amongst the most spectacular in the world. The tremendous flow of water is, of course, eroding the lip of the falls. Geologists

Is evolution bunk?

have measured the rate of erosion: the falls were retreating up the Niagara River at the rate of 1.7 metres (5 feet) per year, until diversion of the water for power generation slowed the rate of erosion in recent times. Since the falls were first formed they have created the Niagara Gorge. This extends downstream from the falls for 11 kilometres (7 miles). It is not too difficult to calculate the date when the falls began. If the rate of erosion has been constant from the beginning, the falls were created about 7,000 years ago; but, of course, if the rocks were much softer when the erosion began, the time is much shorter.

Now let us go down to the sea. The sea is salty, but not as salty as it ought to be if the Earth were 4.5 billion years old. The Earth's rivers carry not only solid sediments into the oceans, but also small quantities of salt, dissolved out of the rocks and soil. By measuring the concentration of salt in river water and multiplying by the time the rivers have been running into the sea, it is possible to calculate how salty the sea ought to be. Even assuming that all the seas started off as fresh water, a most unlikely assumption, if the earth were 4.5 billion years old the seas would now be as saturated with salt as the Dead Sea, and would be as dead. There is no known way in which enough salt from the sea is being lost to maintain a constant level of salinity; once the salt is in the sea, in the sea most of it stays. So this whole process of the salination of the sea has not been going on for billions of years.

Helium is an inert gas; it does not combine with other chemical elements. It is present in very small quantities in the air. Helium is constantly being produced by the decay of two metallic elements in the rocks, uranium and thorium. The helium then diffuses through the crystalline lattice of the rocks. The problem with helium, if the Earth is millions of years old, is twofold: there is too much helium trapped in the rocks and too little out in the atmosphere. As uranium decays it produces both helium and lead.

The Young Earth: 1

Measuring the ratios of uranium and lead in the rocks is a favourite way for scientists to estimate their age. Using this method, scientists often come up with ages of more than a billion years. The problem is that most of the helium produced by this radioactive decay is still there in the rocks in which it was formed. If the rocks are as old as the scientists say, this helium should have diffused out of the rocks long ago, and there should be correspondingly more helium in the atmosphere. The distribution of helium on Earth argues for a much younger planet.

This should also alert us to the frailty of radiometric methods of dating. Several such methods are in use: they depend on the radioactive decay of certain elements such as uranium to lead, potassium to argon and carbon 14 to nitrogen 14. To use these decay processes as a method for dating, however, involves a whole raft of basic assumptions, none of which is verifiable. Different methods often produce vastly different dates for the same rock or fossil. Using a variety of radiometric methods to date a sample of rock from the Mount St Helens lava dome, for example, produced a variety of dates from 0.3 million years to 3 million years old. In fact, everyone had seen that rock being formed just 10 years before.

Carbon 14 has a 'half-life' of 5,700 years; that means that after 5,700 years half the carbon 14 trapped in an organic or inorganic compound will have decayed away. After a mere 57,000 years the amount of carbon 14 in such a compound should be less than one thousandth of the original amount, or virtually undetectable. The trouble is that coal, oil and diamonds, which are supposed to have been formed in the earth millions, if not billions of years ago, still contain significant quantities of carbon 14. If the method of carbon-dating is sound, then coal, oil and diamonds were formed, not ages ago, but comparatively recently.

Is evolution bunk?

Now it is time for a trip to the moon. George Darwin, the son of the famous Charles, rather unhelpfully for his father's cause, discovered that the moon is in fact spiraling away from the Earth at the rate of about 4 centimetres (1.5 inches) per year. It does not seem very much, but if we are looking around for billions of years to leave time for evolution and the deposition of the sedimentary rocks, it is a killer. As little as 1.3 billion years ago the moon would have been near enough to the Earth to be within touching distance. On the other hand, if the moon had been at a sensible distance from the Earth 1.3 billion years ago, it would now be out of sight altogether. Either way, this has not been going on for very long.

There is another problem out there in space: comets. Comets are no more than gigantic snowballs – dust and grit bound together in a ball of ice. The tails which we see streaming away from comets as they orbit the sun are due to the ice melting and the comet leaving behind part of its mass. Comets are part of the solar system, revolving in very eccentric orbits around the sun. Halley's comet reappears once every 76 years. But it will not do so for much longer. One day it will all have melted and gone. If the solar system is 4.5 billion years old, there should not be any comets left at all. So scientists who believe in an old Earth have proposed that the supply of comets is replenished from a place called the Kuiper Belt beyond the orbit of Neptune. Astronomers have indeed identified a number of small objects in this region, but there are nothing like enough of them. Other scientists, like Jan Oort, have invented something called the Oort Cloud, which is supposed to exist even further away beyond the planets. This is another sort of celestial dressing room where comets wait their turn to come in to bat. It is a nice idea, but so far no one has actually seen the Oort Cloud, and it probably belongs with the other fairies at the bottom of the garden.

24

THE YOUNG EARTH: 2

The history of a people or a culture begins with their contemporary written records. Cavemen made wonderful paintings on the walls of their caves, such as those at Lascaux in France, but that does not constitute history. The cavemen and their paintings are prehistoric. Agriculture means people tilling the soil and planting, harvesting and storing the crops, as opposed to living from hand to mouth by hunting and gathering like the cavemen. Civilisation means people living in cities, as opposed to caves, or even villages where they rely on subsistence agriculture as in much of Africa. Civilisation in fact depends on agricultural surpluses which can be stored and shared with a population of non-agricultural workers, in an economy which can afford a more specialised division of labour. In certain fertile regions of the Middle East, civilisation, agriculture and writing all seem to have begun at roughly the same time.

Agriculture is thought to have begun in the Fertile Crescent, from modern Iraq round to Turkey and the Eastern Mediterranean. The oldest civilisations in the world also grew up in the same area, in the Nile delta and the valley of the Tigris and Euphrates in Mesopotamia. The civilisations of ancient Egypt and Sumer produced the oldest written records to have survived, in the form of clay tablets and inscriptions on stone. These civilisations began

Is evolution bunk?

about 3000 BC. Ancient Chinese civilisation is dated somewhat later, around 2000 BC. Evolutionists differ about how long they reckon that *Homo sapiens* has been around – some would say half a million years, others only 150,000. Whichever figure we accept, however, this raises serious questions: what were our ancestors doing all that time, and why do we dig up so few of their skeletons?

The essence of *Homo sapiens* is his large brain, lack of hair, upright posture and the ability to make and use tools. By definition our *Homo sapiens* ancestors were biologically the same as us. So why did they not use their brains as we do? Why did they not use tools as we do? Why did they not get up and go as we do? Why did it take so long for intelligent, skilful human beings to develop agriculture, to build cities, to invent the wheel and to start writing? And what happened to them all when they died? On the other hand, if the Flood receded and people started to repopulate the Earth about 5,000 years ago, it is no surprise that the oldest civilisations and the oldest written records, not forgetting the oldest trees, are all about 5,000 years old. And if Noah's Ark came to rest on the mountains of Ararat in eastern Turkey, it is no surprise that agriculture and the most ancient civilisations also originated in the same part of the world.

Studies of the growth of the human population also confirm these estimates. Population increases by geometrical rather than arithmetical progression – that is to say, by multiplication rather than mere addition. The world's population multiplies by two, it doubles, every so-many years. From the total population of the world today it is a simple mathematical calculation to find out how many times the population has doubled from an original couple: the answer is that we are into the thirty-third doubling. The question is, how many years does it take for the population to double? In the last 150 years the period has been dramatically shortened by improvements in

The Young Earth: 2

medicine, sanitation and diet; world population is now growing faster than ever before. But before 1800, it would not be unreasonable to assume that mortality due to disease, war and famine had remained fairly constant; there are no obvious reasons for it to have changed, at least since the development of agriculture. It is estimated that the population of the world doubled between 1650 and 1850, from about 545 million to 1.1 billion. This 1.1 billion represents 30 doublings. So, suppose we allow 200 years for each doubling, how many years does it take to go back to a total population of eight people, the number who came out of the Ark? The answer is 5,600 years, and 5,600 years before AD 1850 takes us back to 3750 BC!

We can check the accuracy of these calculations against a specific ethnic group of which we have a much more accurate knowledge: the Jews. In 1930, before the Second World War and the Holocaust, the population of world Jewry was about 16 million. This shows that the Jewish population had doubled 24 times. We know that the Jews are descended from Abraham and Sarah, who lived sometime around 2000 BC. We also know a great deal about the history of the Jews, what plagues, wars, famines and persecutions they have faced and survived, and it is surely not less than the rest of mankind. If we say that their descendants have doubled 24 times in 4,000 years, then each doubling took just 166 years. What these calculations all show is that human beings have not been living on the Earth for hundreds of thousands of years. If they had been, it is an even greater mystery what they were doing all that time: not only were they not cultivating the soil, living in cities, inventing the wheel, or writing it all down, they were not even having babies.

Finally, we can consider that most characteristic of all human attributes, language. Evolutionists believe that language started with grunts: our ancestors grunted more and more articulately until they invented words for things.

Is evolution bunk?

The process is supposed to be recapitulated in the development of the child. The baby starts by goo-ing and gurgling; then it starts to say 'mama' and 'dada'. The next stage is to identify objects and people with a single word, and by about the age of two, the baby starts putting words together in simple sentences. From then on, mastery of language increases until the baby can write books about evolution, like this. Prehistorically, then, language is supposed to have increased in complexity with human evolution. From single words for physical objects, languages developed not only a sophisticated vocabulary, but also a grammar and a syntax that became increasingly subtle and expressive of different shades of meaning.

The actual history of known languages, however, shows exactly the opposite development. Just as the known story of the species is one, not of the evolution of new species, but of the extinction of many of the old, so also the known story of language is one, not of increasing complexity and subtlety, but of increasing simplicity and the loss of distinctions that were previously possible. Take the case of Greek. Ancient Greek, of which a rich and varied literature survives, was spoken and written from the fourteenth century to the third century BC. It was a highly complex and inflected language. Its nouns and adjectives declined in five cases and three numbers, singular, dual and plural; its verbs conjugated in six persons. Its verbs had not only an active and a passive voice, but also a middle voice, not only an indicative, imperative and subjunctive mood, but also an optative mood. There were four past tenses: imperfect, perfect, pluperfect and aorist. As well as letters of the alphabet, ancient Greek had breathings and accents which also modified the pronunciation and meaning. To us it seems like some linguistic nightmare. Modern Greek, on the other hand, has lost two cases and one number, the dual, in its nouns, and the middle voice and the optative mood in its verbs; the perfect and pluperfect tenses are

The Young Earth: 2

now expressed by compound verbs instead of conjugations of the main verb; and the inflections of tone have been lost in its pronunciation. Sanskrit, likewise, one of the oldest of the Indo-European languages, spoken in north-west India in 1500 BC, was highly complex and inflected, but has become much simpler in modern Hindustani.

We can see that same process at work in English, even in our own lifetime: a process of the loss of subtlety and shades of meaning. A little phrase that is often heard when people are giving advice is, 'If I were you. . .' Except that nowadays what is more often heard is, 'If I was you. . .'. 'I were' is almost the last living specimen of the English present subjunctive. 'I was' has nothing to do with it at all, being the imperfect indicative: I never was, and I never will be, you. With 'I were' we are losing a nuance or subtlety in the language which cannot be expressed in any other way. So the process that we see at work in human language could be said to be devolutionary! The language of Chaucer and Shakespeare has become, 'I am like oh my God really really cool, man'.

In the last two chapters we have looked at many different signs in the world around us and in recorded history which point not to an Earth or to a race which is hundreds of thousands or millions of years old, but rather to an Earth and a race which is only thousands of years old. It is extraordinary and it must be significant that so many lines of enquiry, from tree-rings to population growth, point to a period about 5,000 years ago as a time when life on Earth, if not began, at least began again. It is somewhere here that we should place the Flood.

Is evolution bunk?

25

WHAT DO THE SCIENTISTS THINK?

The impression which is given to schoolchildren and to the general public is that all real scientists think the same: that they believe in the theory of evolution as we have been examining it and all its ramifications in the chapters above. The impression is also given that anyone who disagrees with this is in the same category as those mythical people who think that the Earth is flat. This impression is perpetuated by the BBC's Natural History Department and its science correspondents. Probably no institution has done more to popularise the theory of evolution and to keep it alive than the BBC, with its block-buster wildlife series and the steady drip of evolutionary stories in the news. The mystery is why the BBC, which preserves a legendary impartiality and objectivity in its reporting of politics and current affairs, behaves like the Ministry of Propaganda for Darwin and Lyell when it comes to natural history and science. The objective truth is that not all scientists think the same.

Fred Hoyle once remarked, 'I have always thought it curious that, while most scientists claim to eschew religion, it actually dominates their thoughts more than it does the clergy.' That will be news to most people, I suspect, but I myself do not find it at all surprising. It may be a sad reflection on the clergy (to whom we will come in the next chapter), but by the very nature of their

Is evolution bunk?

profession scientists are constantly studying the works of God. Whether they understand it or not, while scientists are exploring the mysteries of the universe or unravelling the secrets of DNA they are contemplating the handiwork of the Almighty. It is hardly surprising, then, if God dominates their thoughts. That is not to say that all scientists believe in God, far from it, but they cannot help thinking about the spiritual issues that science raises. All are aware that the background to their work is the long-standing controversy between the theory of evolution and the theory of creation, a controversy which is still very much alive today. So whether they take an evolutionist position or a creationist position themselves, scientists are all wrestling with the same ultimate questions: Where have we come from? Why are we here? What is the meaning of life?

The truth is that many scientists are indeed evolutionists, of one sort or another. The problems involved with the original, gradualist form of Darwinism, some of which we have examined in the preceding chapters, are so great that many biologists have now abandoned it in favour of some modified form of Darwinism. Two current alternatives which are being tried for size are 'punctuated equilibrium' and 'directed evolution'. Michael Denton, whose books I have referred to earlier, is specifically not a creationist: he believes that nature shows every sign of having been designed with a certain destiny in mind, but he is not arguing for the existence of God. Michael Behe, on the other hand, is a Roman Catholic believer, but the conclusions that he has reached from his research into biochemical mechanisms have been dictated not by his faith, but by his science. These two scientists, and others, would be recognised as proponents of intelligent design, but would not thereby identify themselves as creationists.

Creationist scientists, however, there are. John Ashton has edited a book called *In Six Days*, which is a series of

What do the scientists think?

short essays by 50 scientists who believe in the biblical story of creation in every detail, and who find nothing in their science that cannot be reconciled with their faith. These scientists are drawn from every discipline: biology, chemistry, physics, geology, zoology, astronomy, and include those working in both pure research and applied engineering. They come from all over the world, from the USA, Canada, Australia, South Africa, New Zealand and the United Kingdom.

Some have started and finished with an unshakeable faith in the literal truth of the book of Genesis; others were actually converted to Christianity by their study of science. Stephen C. Meyer, the director of the Center for Science and Culture at the Discovery Institute in Seattle, USA, registers around 400 scientists who subscribe to the idea of intelligent design. It is important to emphasise that these are not Mickey Mouse scientists: they have as many degrees from as many prestigious universities as anyone else; they hold as many professorships as anyone else; they have published as many learned articles in the scientific journals as anyone else; and many of them are world leaders in their specialist fields; their creationist beliefs do not hinder their scientific researches – indeed, they would claim that they assist them.

There is really very little correlation between scientific expertise and religious belief. Some scientists are evolutionists, others are creationists; some are theists, others are atheists; some are Christians and evolutionists, others are Christians and creationists. The reader may like to reflect on the fact that many of the scientists whose views and discoveries I have quoted in this book are not believers; Stephen Hawking, Martin Rees, Fred Hoyle, Roger Penrose, Paul Davies and Michael Denton are not Christians, and certainly not creationists. Yet their questions and their conclusions have pointed us in the direction which we have followed in these chapters – a

Is evolution bunk?

direction in which they themselves seem unwilling to go. Even Richard Dawkins gives the game away in the titles which he gives his own books: *Climbing Mount Improbable* and *The Blind Watchmaker*. There may be blind piano-tuners, but there are no blind watchmakers.

The point is that faith is not dictated by science. Scientific integrity does not demand that everyone must be an evolutionist. Indeed, there comes a tipping point in the accumulation of scientific evidence where scientific integrity demands that we seriously question evolutionism and seriously investigate creationism, and it is the contention of this book, and of many scientists, that this point has now been reached.

* * *

There was a fourteenth-century schoolman called William of Ockham who enunciated a philosophical and scientific principle which has become known as Ockham's Razor. It states that 'Entities should not be multiplied unnecessarily.' It has been invoked in the past by evolutionists to discount God as an explanation for nature. God was an entity that we did not need; the world was self-explanatory. But the more that science has advanced, the less self-explanatory the world has become. It seems that we cannot explain the universe without postulating some other entity or entities. Creationists postulate one additional entity, God. Evolutionists are being forced to postulate all sorts of other additional entities, none of which have been discovered, and some of which are essentially beyond discovery. Here is a list of some of these entities that we have met in this book:

What do the scientists think?

- *Dark matter and dark energy.* This is a very large 'entity' indeed: 95% of the universe. The equations that astrophysicists have used to explain the Big Bang do not add up, unless there is vastly more matter and energy in the universe than we can actually see. So they postulate the existence of 'dark matter and dark energy'. No one has seen dark matter, and perhaps no one can see dark matter. Scientists have been looking for it in vain. No one even understands what dark energy means.
- *Multiple universes.* Those who want to cling on to a naturalistic view of existence have to invent whole universes to explain the precise conditions which enable our universe to exist. They are essentially unknowable to us in this universe. These entities never ought to be allowed to pass the test of Ockham's Razor.
- *Panspermia.* There are living organisms that evolved on some other rock in the universe and hitched a lift to Earth on a meteorite. No one has ever seen one.
- *Missing links.* If living organisms evolved by a process of gradual change, as evolutionary theory suggests, then transitional forms between major groups ought to be common. As it happens, transitional fossils are rare, especially among the groups with the best fossil record, the invertebrates.

A great deal of scientific time and effort, not to mention money, goes into trying to find these entities. When these efforts fail, they remain as articles of faith, like fairies at the bottom of the garden, for without them the theory of evolution falls to the ground. Ockham's Razor tells us not to multiply entities unnecessarily. The evolutionists seem to multiply entities in all directions. The creationists rely on just one. The entities that evolutionists need to explain

Is evolution bunk?

the universe all seem very remote from the real world, while the only entity that the creationists need is God, 'who is not far from each one of us, for in him we live and move and have our being' (see Acts 17:27–28).

26

WHAT DO THE CHRISTIANS THINK?

The general impression may be that all Christians believe in the theory of creation as we have defined it in this book. But just as the impression that all scientists believe in evolution is mistaken, so the impression that all Christians believe in creation, in this sense, is also mistaken. The answer to 'What do the Christians think?' is that generally Christians think about this issue as little as possible.

In the nineteenth century, churchmen put up a stout rearguard action against the theory of evolution, but by the twentieth century most of them had come to regard the battle as lost. Only a few, like Arthur Rendle-Short, kept the creationist flag flying. Those who did so clung doggedly to a literalist belief in the inerrancy of Scripture: what is commonly but unhelpfully called fundamentalism. They believed that if the Bible said it was true, then it must be true, whatever evidence to the contrary science might produce. For Christians who knew the Bible well but did not know very much science, this was probably not too difficult, but for those like Rendle-Short, who knew both equally well, it involved a lifetime of intellectual travail and a decision to suspend judgement in the hope that the future would shed more light. How the scientists of the twenty-first century, who have produced such compelling evidence of intelligent design and irreducible complexity, would have rejoiced his heart and satisfied his soul.

Is evolution bunk?

For the most part, other Christians, with the honourable motive of preserving their intellectual integrity, looked for ways of accommodating the old religion to the new science, or even of divorcing the two. The six days of creation in the book of Genesis were extended to millions of years to accommodate the geological ages and the time required for evolution. The latest scientific theories were accepted as the framework for discussion, and Christian doctrine was adjusted to fit them.

Today, scientists and theologians coming from a scientific background, like Denis Alexander, Alistair McGrath and John Polkinghorne, often continue this tradition and try to incorporate the latest developments in naturalistic theory into their theology. Another approach to the problem is to say that science and religion are two different, non-overlapping magisteria, or types of knowledge: science tells us 'how', while religion tells us 'why'. But there has always been a profound incoherence about these attempts to adapt Christian doctrine to, or divorce Christian doctrine from, evolutionary theory. It is not just the facile argument that if you cannot trust the first few chapters of the Bible, why should you trust any of it; it is a doctrinal incoherence.

Christian doctrine asserts that there is something unique about mankind: we alone are made in the image of God. Yet if the species form a continuum from the algae in the pond to the chimpanzees and humans, where are the grounds for our uniqueness? We are no more than naked apes. Furthermore, Christian doctrine has always emphasised the important role of sin, of humanity's rebellion against God, as the ultimate explanation of suffering and death.

It was for this that Christ came and died on the cross, to redeem and save our race from sin. But if mankind is the result of evolution, then long before humans appeared, the animals were suffering and dying, preying and being

What do the Christians think?

preyed upon, and humans simply joined them in the selfish struggle for survival. It is hardly surprising if most of the clergy have, from one year's end to the next, avoided teaching and preaching about creation and the Fall in any historical sense. For 100 years both clergy and laity have avoided the subject of creation and evolution, feeling inadequate to the task of either understanding or arguing about it. Most people who become Christians today do so because they are attracted to the person of Jesus Christ and are persuaded of his claims about himself and his claim upon their lives.

It is indicative of the church's attitude to the subject of this book that the most successful tool of evangelism today, the Alpha Course, avoids creation altogether and starts with the question, 'Who is Jesus?' The historic creeds of the church begin with a statement of faith about the Creator; today we begin with the man, Jesus of Nazareth. In the circumstances it is the only strategy.

For 150 years the theory of evolution has been like an elephant in the church's sitting room. At the beginning the church made strenuous efforts to keep the elephant out. When these failed, the church resigned itself to living with the elephant. Adjustments were made to accommodate its presence; people found ways of navigating around it. It was certainly an embarrassment, especially when entertaining visitors; it was hoped that if we did not draw attention to it, the visitors would not notice that it was there. The family became so accustomed to its presence, like you do, that they ceased to think that it was odd. They even came to be fond of the beast, and to be proud of the stratagems that they had devised for living with it. Certainly, it has been a long time since anyone seriously thought of moving the elephant out; it was just too big.

Now, all of a sudden, it seems much less difficult. Now it is the evolutionists who find they have an unwelcome

Is evolution bunk?

guest in the sitting room. Michael Behe has described the evidence for intelligent design in exactly the same way: as an elephant in a roomful of scientists. Now it is the scientists rather than the Christians who are wondering how to deal with an unwanted intruder, because while one side of the elephant may be labelled 'intelligent design', the other side might be labelled 'God'. Michael Behe writes:

> 'The result of these cumulative efforts to investigate the cell is a loud and piercing cry of 'design!' The result is so unambiguous and so significant that it must be ranked as one of the greatest achievements in the history of science ... The observation of the intelligent design of life is as momentous as the observation that the earth goes around the sun ... This triumph of science should evoke cries of 'Eureka!' from ten thousand throats, should occasion much hand-slapping and high-fiving, and perhaps even an excuse for a day off. But no bottles have been uncorked, no hands slapped. Instead, a curious, embarrassed silence surrounds the stark complexity of the cell. When the subject comes up in public, feet start to shuffle, and breathing gets a bit laboured. In private, people are a bit more relaxed; many explicitly admit the obvious but then stare at the ground, shake their heads, and let it go at that.'[22]

The elephant is on the move, whether people like it or not. After 150 years he is thinking of changing his address and embarrassing the evolutionists instead.

---

[22] Michael Behe, *Darwin's Black Box*, The Free Press, 1996, pp. 232–3.

27

THE CREATOR

The existence of the universe demands a Creator. The precision of the physical forces of the universe, the coincidence of so many favourable factors on this planet, the extraordinary properties of the elements, like carbon and water, found in such abundance on the Earth, the complexity of the living cell, the language of DNA, the ingenuity of the molecular machines on which life depends, the utility of the limbs and organs of the different species for their function, all these things demand a Designer and a Maker. Who, then, is this Designer, Maker and Creator?

We can tell a certain amount about him from the things which have been made. We can tell that this is a person and not an 'it', because design presupposes an intelligence, a mind and a will. He alone is uncreated. He is unimaginably great, in understanding and in power. It is a reasonable deduction that he himself delights in his creation. For no apparent purpose other than sheer delight, he paints a different sunset every evening on the canvas of the sky; he covers the trees and hedgerows with blossoms in the spring, and in autumn he turns the woods to red and gold.

It is difficult to think of an evolutionary explanation for the existence of beauty: what is the survival value of a sunset sky or the colours of an autumn leaf? It is said that, 'Beauty is in the eye of the beholder.' That is true, but it is

Is evolution bunk?

not the eye of the beholder that is beautiful, but the thing beheld. The existence of beauty demands the existence of a Beholder. The Creator is not only a craftsman, but an artist who creates not merely for utility, but for enjoyment. He makes many a rose to bloom and many a bird to soar, which he alone will ever see. If we delight in these things too, we only share in their Creator's joy.

But what shall we say of the other side of life? All the animals that are born, are born as we are, to die. Some of them, like some of us, will die slow and painful deaths. Pestilence and disease, earthquake and famine rob many of God's creatures, not least the human race, of a full span of life, and often make that lifespan nasty, brutish and short. Besides all these things, the human race brings upon itself untold misery and poverty through its greed and lust and violence. If it is God's world, then God is responsible for this mountain of suffering, for allowing it, if not for creating it himself. What sort of a God is this? Is he benevolent or malevolent? Does he care?

These are questions that human beings have asked themselves since the dawn of time; our hopes and fears have always been focused not just on the next meal, but on what sort of a God or gods are dealing with us and how we are to deal with them. People have sought answers to these questions in many different ways: by offering prayers and sacrifices, by practising magic, by the mortification of their bodily desires. The truth is that none of these things brings us any closer to an understanding of God. Human beings by their own efforts cannot discover the nature of the One with whom they have to do. How could they? What is mankind in the immensity of the universe? A tiny speck on a lonely planet. How can we understand or what can we know of our Creator? Unless, that is, our Creator chooses to disclose himself and his purposes to us, his creatures.

The Creator

There is one faith in the world which claims that God has done precisely that.

> In many and various ways God spoke of old to our fathers by the [Hebrew] prophets; but in these last days he has spoken to us by a Son, whom he appointed the heir of all things, through whom also he created the world. (Hebrews 1:1–2 RSV)

God has revealed himself, through his words and through his works: through his word which he spoke to Abraham, to Moses and the prophets of the Old Testament; through the works which he did for his Chosen People, leading them out of slavery in Egypt and into the Promised Land. Above all, God has revealed himself in the person of his Son Jesus: in his words and teaching, and in his miracles of healing and deliverance. Finally, he revealed himself in the death of his Son for our salvation and in his resurrection from the dead. Christianity is revelation; it is not the outcome of humanity's search for enlightenment. It was not mediated by angels or spirits, but by God himself, who in the person of his Son became a man alongside us, and shared our human life from the womb to the tomb.

In Jesus we see that God is love. It is not his will that any should perish. He knows when a sparrow falls to the ground. Even the hairs of our head are numbered. However many of us there may be on Earth, he knows and cares for each one; each one is precious in his sight, from the unborn child to the oldest granny. In all our affliction, he is afflicted. We are his. 'He has made us for himself, and our hearts are restless till they find their rest in him.' (St Augustine)

We are his. This is a source, first, of inexpressible comfort, second, an invitation to seek him for ourselves, and third, an inescapable claim on our obedience. The first,

Is evolution bunk?

many are glad to accept; the second, not so many perhaps are willing to pursue; the third presents problems for us all. This is the root of human sin, an incurable inclination towards our own autonomy. Frank Sinatra boasted of what is our common shame: 'I did it my way.' God made us to do it his way, to live our lives his way. His is a better way than any way we can ever devise for ourselves, yet we persist in the original sin of Adam and Eve in doing it our own way, thinking that we know best. Each one of us reproduces the sin of Adam, and each one of us inherits the consequences of the disobedience of the whole human race.

God will not change his mind. If we persist in our sin, then we will have to endure the consequences. The novelist Barbara Kingsolver wrote with great percipience in her novel *The Poisonwood Bible*, 'God does not have to punish us. He just lets us live long enough to punish ourselves.' The judgement of God is simply that he does not change; it is we who must do the changing. This is the meaning of repentance: a recognition that my life is not my own; I have a Creator to whom I am accountable for what I have done and what I shall do, and I must change if I am to enjoy the good things which he has prepared for me in this world and the next.

28

SUFFERING AND REDEMPTION

The creation has become a battleground. We live with the endless wars between tribes and nations, between religions and ideologies, between the oppressors and the oppressed. But beyond all that there is a spiritual warfare: the battle between light and darkness, between good and evil, between truth and the lie, between God and 'that ancient serpent, who is called the Devil and Satan, the deceiver of the whole world' (Revelation 12:9 RSV). The most dangerous and vicious of human wars occur when one or both sides identify themselves with the cause of God and their opponents with the devil. The truth is that the front line in this battle runs through the middle of every nation and every human heart. But the recognition of the reality of this spiritual warfare is essential to an understanding of the world in which we live.

God made a world that was good, in which there was no disease, no famine, no earthquakes, no death. The creation was in harmony with itself, humanity with the animals and the environment, and the animals with one another. The first human couple, together with the whole creation, were in harmony with God, a harmony for which they were created. Disharmony entered the world when this couple sinned, disobeyed God, rebelled against his order in the world. At that moment war in heaven became war on Earth. Envy, anger, avarice and lust disrupted human

Is evolution bunk?

relationships; fear spread like a plague through God's creatures; killing and being killed became a way of life. Today 'the whole world is in the power of the evil one' (1 John 5:19 RSV). Earthquakes, pestilence and famine, war, crime and addiction, even death itself, were not part of God's original plan for the world. Something has gone wrong with God's creation. These things are the works of the evil one.

This is not to say that the two sides in the spiritual battle are equal. God is the only true god; all other spiritual beings, though they may be called gods and worshipped as gods, are created spirits. God alone is almighty. The battle is the result of spiritual envy of God, a desire to take God's place, a desire that infected the heart of Satan and infects the human heart whenever we aspire to autonomy. There are mysteries about the ways of God, which we can recognise even if we cannot understand them. One of these is free will. God has given to both angels and human beings the gift of free will: it is the freedom to obey or to disobey. God is love; he made his creatures for love, to love him and to love one another. Love is tested and made real in obedience. The mayhem and suffering that we see and experience in the world around us is the result of disobedience, angelic disobedience and our own.

God, however, is not going to surrender either his creation or his purpose to another. God perseveres. He sees and knows the sufferings of his people and of his creation, and he has come to their aid. The Bible tells the story not only of creation and of human disobedience, but of the steps that God has taken to restore his world and his people to himself. He chose a man, Abraham, and after testing his obedience, promised that he would be a source of blessing to the whole world. Through the descendants of Abraham God prepared a nation from which would come a Redeemer and a Saviour for all mankind. From Abraham, through Jesus, to today, the call of God to each of

Suffering and redemption

us is to repent of our sin, to believe in him, and to obey his will. He does not will the death of sinners, but rather that sinners turn from their wickedness and live. God's métier is to forgive; he is the God of the new beginning and the fresh start, for individuals and for the world.

But God is also just, and how can God justly overlook misdeeds which have brought suffering and loss to others? Justice demands recompense and punishment; it is not just or fair that evildoers should go unpunished. We are entitled to forgive those who have hurt us; we are not entitled to forgive those who have hurt others. So God came and suffered himself; he came into a suffering world and experienced suffering himself. God cannot be accused of not caring what we suffer; he knows it at first hand. Jesus, as the Son of God, suffered rejection, scorn, condemnation, extreme pain, violence and death. On the cross Jesus was earning the right to forgive anyone for anything. Looked at from the point of view of God's justice, God in Christ took the punishment for the world's sins upon himself. On the cross God took responsibility for all the consequences of creating people with a free will, and for all the sin and suffering in the world.

But the cross is not the end of the story of Jesus, or of God's dealings with the world. Jesus was raised from the dead by the power of God. Of no other human being in history has this seriously been said. But Jesus 'showed himself to [his followers] and gave many convincing proofs that he was alive . . . over a period of forty days' (Acts 1:3). The Christian faith depends from first to last on the truth of the resurrection of Jesus from the dead. But it is a fact as firmly based and authenticated as any event in history. And this same Jesus, alive, has been encountered and is still being encountered in the Spirit in a life-changing way by millions of human beings down the ages and across the world today.

Is evolution bunk?

The resurrection of Jesus is the beginning of a new creation. Out of the death of the old creation God is bringing a new one. In the new creation God's vision and purpose for the old will be perfected. The sufferings of this life will seem but a slight momentary affliction compared to the weight of glory which we shall enjoy for eternity. There will be no more death, no more crying or mourning or pain, for all these things will have passed away. We may often question, here and now, whether anything can justify the misery and pain of the world, not just human pain but the pain of all God's sentient creatures. There is a mystery about this also. But, in the end, God's answer to this question is 'Yes'.

29

THE REAPPEARANCE OF GOD

Chance has had its chance. Jacques Monod's thesis was that 'Chance alone is at the source of every innovation, of all creation in the biosphere; pure chance, absolutely free but blind, at the very root of the stupendous edifice of evolution' (see p. 69). If the universe is held to be self-explanatory, then everything is just pure chance. But those who appeal to chance must allow their chances to be calculated by those who are competent to do so. The mathematician Roger Penrose has calculated the chances of the physical constants of the universe being what they are by chance. Result: no chance.

The astronomer Fred Hoyle calculated the chances of life arising on Earth spontaneously. Result: no chance. Francis Crick, who with James Watson discovered DNA, came to the same conclusion: 'An honest man, armed with all the knowledge available to us now, could only state that in some sense, the origin of life appears at the moment to be almost a miracle.'[23] Even Richard Dawkins, the high priest of Darwinism, admits that evolution is 'improbable'. Chance is simply not up to the job. The disappearance of chance is the reappearance of God.

It is not in the nature of science to provide proof; science provides evidence which tends either to support or to

---

[23] Francis Crick, *Life Itself*, Simon and Schuster, 1981, p. 88.

Is evolution bunk?

refute a theory. We have examined two theories for the origin of the universe, of life and of the species, and of the Earth as we know it today: the theory of evolution and the theory of creation. A few years ago the case for the theory of evolution seemed to most people to be cut and dried. Then, with new discoveries particularly in the field of molecular biology, the case began to seem much less certain. As time has passed, the evidence supporting the theory of evolution has begun to trickle away, like the sand in an egg-timer, until today evolution seems to be no more than a temporary delusion. On the other hand, evidence to support the theory of creation has been steadily building up, to the point at which I, for one, am convinced that it is true.

But I would not want to claim on the basis of science alone that the case for creation is cut and dried either. There are many questions still to be answered, and I can probably enumerate as many of them as can those who disagree with me. What about crocodiles' teeth? It does not look as if they were designed for eating spinach. What about the light from the stars? It seems to have taken millions of years to reach us. But we have to remember that for the last 150 years almost all science has been done within the evolutionary paradigm.

It is necessary to examine each piece of evidence and each assumption afresh in the light of a new paradigm, that of creation. But when all is said and done, the sheer quantity of knowledge involved, increasing all the time as research advances, across such a wide range of disciplines, seems to me to mean that no one is ever going to be able to absorb and correlate all the relevant information, and it seems that as some issues are resolved, new ones emerge which prevent a conclusive answer being given. The whole universe, as we see it today and as we explore its past, is so full of riddles and enigmas that certainly at present no one can seriously claim to have all the answers.

The reappearance of God

But all these are questions of detail. When we look at the fundamental questions, as we have done in this book ...

1. the very existence of the universe,
2. the fundamental forces of the universe,
3. the properties of the Earth and water,
4. the origin of life,
5. the ubiquitous phenomenon of irreducible complexity,
6. the mystery of the information stored in DNA,

... we see that the theory of evolution is unable to answer them. The problems for the theory of evolution are not just a few gaps in the evidence, they are conceptual ones. On the other hand, to these really big, conceptual questions that we have examined, the theory of creation can provide answers which are coherent and satisfying both to the mind and to the heart. Let us remind ourselves of where we started (see above, pp. 21-22):

> There is a God. By his word the universe was made. He spoke and it was done. He created light. He created the sun, moon and stars. He created the Earth. He created the land and the sea. He created fish to swim in the sea and birds to fly in the air, each according to its kind. He created the plants and the trees. He created the animals each according to its kind. Last he created man. He did all this in a short period of time, say, a week, and not so long ago, say, less than 10,000 years. What God created was good, and for a while peace and harmony reigned on the Earth. Then something went wrong, and gradually everything fell apart.

Is evolution bunk?

Fear and suspicion reigned on the Earth; animals and people started to kill each other, disease and death ruled the world. So God decided to start again. He sent a worldwide flood, breaking up the crust of the earth, releasing water from the atmosphere in the form of rain and water from under the earth in subterranean reservoirs. A man called Noah and his family, together with specimens of all kinds of creatures, survived the flood in a large boat, and from them the world was repopulated, say 5,000 years ago.

At the end of the day, we are left with a decision between two faiths – faith in evolution, or faith in God – as the explanation of the world. How we evaluate the two theories that we have examined will depend more on our attitude to the idea of God than on the scientific evidence. Richard Dawkins does not want to believe in God, so it is unlikely that any evidence is ever going to convince him. What people need in the end is not more arguments, but more experience of God.

I said earlier in the book, 'The God who made the world in which we actually live is essentially knowable, a God with whom we can interact, a God who makes himself known to us through the things which he has made, and who gives meaning and purpose to our lives.' If you, dear reader, have reached this point in the book and you want to know God for yourself, I assure you that he is as anxious to meet you as you are to meet him.

The best way that I know for you to make his acquaintance, and to begin a personal relationship with him, is for you to enrol for the Alpha Course. The Alpha Course will introduce you to Jesus, who is 'the radiance of God's glory and the exact representation of his being, sustaining all things by his powerful word' (Hebrews 1:3).

The reappearance of God

Jesus will reveal God to you and enable you to be reconciled to him, whatever you may have done. He will also give you a life which will last for ever.

Wherever you live in the world there is probably an Alpha Course within reach of you. So go to www.alpha.org and click on 'Find a course'.

Is evolution bunk?

30

FINAL THOUGHTS

The following extract is taken from *Nuffield Science, Pupil's Book 13 to 16 Years Old*, Unit: 'Evolution'.

> There are many people who would accept the four observations on which Darwin based his theory of evolution by natural selection and which we have explored in this book.
> These observations were:
>
> > The enormous number of offspring that organisms are capable of producing.
> > The variation which exists in organisms.
> > The inheritance of some of these variations.
> > The effect of the environment.
>
> But many people would not agree that this all adds up to a theory of evolution. There could be other explanations of this variety. One explanation is *special creation*; this means that each species was created by God as part of His plan for the Universe. Special creation is not usually mentioned in science textbooks because it is not a scientific explanation; but it is

Is evolution bunk?

something many people believe. Perhaps if we were honest, we would admit that we do not actually *know* how evolution took place, or indeed if it has happened at all. But humans are unique: we have brains, tongues and hands as evidence. We shall always look for explanations for the variety of the living world we see around us. As more and more facts are discovered, it may be that our present ideas will be changed.

Things may have changed since I was at school after all. Michael Brooks, a consultant for *New Scientist* and author of *13 Things That Don't Make Sense* also wrote in a newspaper article:

> Welcome to science in the real world: it is messy, inconclusive, and subject to revision. As the former chief scientific advisor to the government, Lord May, once said, science is best represented as 'organised scepticism' – and science's results and conclusions have to be included in that scepticism. Science is not the arbiter of truth. All it can do is offer opinions about the answers to certain questions that we ask of nature. And it reserves the right to revise those opinions in the light of future discoveries.

I, for one, have revised my opinions since I was at school, in the light of more recent discoveries. I invite you to do the same.

BOOK LIST FOR FURTHER READING

These books are the ones on which I have chiefly relied for the technical information and arguments which I have presented in this book. Not all of their authors are creationists by any means, or even Christians, and they are not of course responsible for the use to which I have put their thoughts. Readers who wish to pursue this subject further, and in particular to acquaint themselves with some of the technicalities, will, however, find these books helpful.

Denis Alexander, *Creation or Evolution,* Monarch 2008

John Ashton (ed.), *In Six Days, why fifty scientists choose to believe in creation*, Master Books, 2001

Michael Behe, *Darwin's Black Box*, The Free Press, 1996

Charles Darwin, *Autobiography*, ed. Gavin de Beer, Oxford University Press, 1983

Paul Davies, *The Mind of God*, Penguin, 1993

—, *The Goldilocks Enigma: Why is the Universe Just Right for Life?* Allen Lane, 2006

Michael Denton, *Evolution: a Theory in Crisis*, Adler and Adler, 1986

—, *Nature's Destiny*, The Free Press, 1998

Anthony Flew, *There Is a God,* Harper 2007

Paul Garner, *The New Creationism,* Evangelical Press, 2009

Stephen Hawking, *A Brief History of Time*, Bantam Press, 1988

Randal Keynes, *Annie's Box, Darwin, his Daughter and Human Evolution*, Fourth Estate, 2001

Is evolution bunk?

Simon Ings, *The Eye, a Natural History*, Bloomsbury 2007

John Lennox, *God's Undertaker,* Lion 2009

Kevin Logan, *Responding to the Challenge of Evolution*, Kingsway, 2002

Stephen C. Meyer, *Signature in the Cell,* Harper 2010

—, *Darwin's Doubts*, Harper 2013

Norman Nevin, *Should Christians Embrace Evolution?* IVP 2009

Roger Penrose, *The Emperor's New Mind*, Oxford University Press, 1989

Fazale Rana, *The Cell's Design,* Baker 2008

John Polkinghorne, *Quarks, Chaos and Christianity*, Triangle, 1994

Martin J. Rees, *Just Six Numbers, the deep forces that shape the universe*, Weidenfeld and Nicholson, 1999

John Rendle-Short, *Green Eye of the Storm*, Banner of Truth Trust, 1998

Ariel Roth, *Origins*, Review and Herald, 1998

Lee Strobel, *The Case for a Creator*, Zondervan, 2004

Roger Trigg, *Philosophy Matters,* Blackwell, 2002

John Whitcomb and Henry Morris, *The Genesis Flood*, Baker Book House, 1961

Carl Zimmer, *Microcosm: E.coli and the new science of life.* Heinemann, 2008

ACKNOWLEDGEMENTS

My friend Paul Garner of the Biblical Creation Society has given me help with the details and arguments in this book. But if there are still factual errors, as there may be, or if the arguments are still fundamentally flawed, that is my fault and not his. The reader will have come to appreciate what a wide range of expertise is necessary to cover this whole subject; no-one is going to get it all right. But, details apart, Paul and I, and many others, are persuaded that the overall thesis of this book is true, and we hope that more and more people will come to know their Creator and Saviour through its pages.

Those who wish to go deeper into the subject, or to keep up with ongoing research, can become members of the Biblical Creation Society, at PO Box 22, Rugby, Warwick CV22 7SY, England. The Society publishes a regular journal called Origins containing material for both the general reader and the more technically minded. Visit their website at www.biblicalcreation.org.uk.

* * *

The illustrations in this book were made on computer by Adam Jackson and derived from material in the public domain on the internet. Visit Adam at www.tomorrownight.com.

Is evolution bunk?

INDEX

Agate Springs, 122
Agriculture, 139-40
Alpha Course, 153, 167
Archaeoraptor, 100
Atheism, 27
Atmosphere, 43, 136-7
Attenborough, David, 28
Augustine, St, 157
Baltic amber deposits, 122
Bananas, 110-111
Bats, 12, 78, 95-6, 103, 106, 138
Beauty, 155-56
Behe, Michael, 60, 146, 154
Bible, 15-16, 21, 29, 125-6, 151-2, 160
Big Bang, 12, 20, 31-2, 149
Binary code, 63-4
Birds, 76-7, 83, 89, 93, 100, 119, 165
Bridging the gaps, 78-9
Burglar alarms, 58-60
Cambrian Explosion, 94-5
Canyons, 121, 128, 132-4
Carbon, 43, 48-9, 123, 137, 155
Catastrophism, 117, 124
Cavemen, 139
Cells, 48, 51-5, 58, 60-2, 64-6, 70, 72, 94, 104, 111, 154, 155
Chimpanzees, 65-6, 110-1, 152
Christian Evolutionists, 16, 152
Cilium, 60-1
Civilisation, 139-40
Cladistics, 96
Classification of living organisms, 75-8, 96
Climbing Mount Improbable, 71, 148

Coal, 59, 123, 127, 134, 137
Columbia Plateau, 115
Comets, 23, 138
Computers, 27, 63-4, 66, 71, 173
Continental drift, 115
Creation, Theory of, 21-2, 55, 69, 72-3, 107, 111, 146, 151, 164-5
Crick, Francis, 163
Cross of Christ, 152, 161
Dark matter and dark energy, 32, 149
Darwin, Charles, 11-12, 20-1, 28, 30, 54, 62, 77-9, 87, 89, 91, 94-5, 99, 103-4, 116, 134, 145, 169
Darwin, George, 138
Davies, Paul, 45, 50, 147
Dawkins, Richard, 27-9, 54-5, 71, 148, 163, 166
Death, 21, 26, 28, 32, 58, 89, 104, 120, 124, 152, 156-7, 159-62, 166
Dembski, William, 39
Denton, Michael, 16, 50, 52, 146-7
Dinosaurs, 100-1, 114, 120, 124, 126
Directed Evolution, 146
Dismal Swamp, 123, 134
Disparity, 94
Diversity, 94
DNA, 51, 61-2, 64-7, 69, 71-2, 87, 89-90, 104, 109-11, 146, 155, 163, 165
Dogs, 76-9, 88, 108, 122
Dust, 119, 138
Earth, 12-15, 17, 20-3, 29, 34, 41-5, 47-9, 53-55, 70-3, 79, 90, 93, 112, 114-5, 119, 122-4, 125-9, 133-4, 135-43, 145, 149, 154, 155, 157, 159, 163-6
Einstein, Albert, 20, 37

Elements, 12, 43, 48, 60, 70, 72, 90, 136-7. 155

Embryos, 11-12, 99-100, 103-9

Entropy, 89-90, 108

Erosion, 113-5, 129, 134, 136

Evolution, Theory of, 11, 14-16, 20, 22, 28-9, 53, 57-8, 62, 65-6, 69, 71, 73, 77, 81, 84, 90-1, 93-6, 99-100, 102-3, 107, 109, 113, 116, 134, 145-6, 149, 151, 153, 164-5, 169

Eyes, 95, 108, 111, 120

Fakes, 99, 101-2

Feathers, 76, 85, 101, 108, 111, 122

Fertile Crescent, 139

Finches, 11, 20, 77-9, 83, 87, 111

First Cause, 34

Fish, 11-12, 21, 48, 76, 83, 89, 93, 99, 114, 119-21, 124, 127, 129, 165

Flood, Noah's, 22, 125-9, 133-5, 140, 143, 166

Fossil graveyards, 122, 127

Fossilization, 119

Fossilized fish, 12, 114, 119-21, 127, 129

Fossilized trees, 122

Fossil record, 12, 84, 93-7, 107-8, 111, 123, 127, 129, 149

Frauds, 99-103, 109

Freaks, 57, 90

Free will, 160-61

Fruit-fly, 57

Fundamentalism, 28, 151

Fundamental forces of the universe, 37-9, 45, 49, 55, 70, 165

Galapagos Islands, 11, 20, 77, 88

Galileo, 15, 20, 30

Garner, Paul, 109

Geiseltal, 122

Gene pool, 87-90

Genes, 27, 53, 57, 60-1, 65-6, 75, 87-91, 103-6, 108-9

Geologic column, 93, 95

God, 13-17, 21, 27-9, 34-5, 40, 54, 69, 72-4, 111, 125-6, 134, 143, 146, 148, 150, 152, 154, 155-62, 163, 165-7, 169

God Delusion, The, 54

Goldilocks factor, 41

Gorges, 132, 136

Gravity, 19-20, 37-8, 43-4

Greek language, 142

Haeckel, Ernst, 11-12, 99, 104, 107, 109

Hawking, Stephen, 32, 70, 147

Helium, 136-7

History, 20, 22, 100, 113, 117, 119, 134, 139, 141-3, 154, 161

Homology, 103-6, 107, 109-10

Hoyle, Fred, 12, 38, 54, 145, 147, 163

Human beings, 14, 75, 77, 79, 87-8, 105, 110-1, 126, 140-1, 156, 160-1

Humanity, 152, 157, 159

Hutton, James, 113

Huxley, Thomas, 27

Ice, 42, 44, 47, 93, 138

Information, 39, 51-2, 63-7, 71-2, 85, 88-91, 108, 111, 164-5

Intelligent Design, 22, 39, 45, 55, 61-2, 79, 106, 110, 112, 146-7, 151, 154

Irreducible Complexity, 55, 57-62, 63, 71, 84-5, 108, 151, 165

Jesus, 153, 157, 160-2, 166-7

Jews, 125, 141

Judgement, 158

Jurassic Morrison Formation, 114, 129

Kingsolver, Barbara, 158

Languages, 52, 141-3, 155

Lascaux, 139
Liakhov Islands, 122
Life, 13-15, 22-3, 28, 37, 41-5, 47-55, 58, 64-7, 70-2, 75, 79, 91, 93-4, 99, 143, 146, 154-8, 164-5
Lungs, 83-4
Lyell, Charles, 113, 116, 119, 134, 145
Mars, 23, 43
McGrath, Alistair, 152
Meyer, Stephen C., 147
Micro-evolution, 79, 116
Miller, Hugh, 120
Missing links, 94, 100-1, 108, 149
Mitochondria, 52, 60-2
Monod, Jacques, 69, 163
Moon, 21, 34, 42-4, 48, 55, 70, 72, 138, 165
Mount Ararat, 140
Mount St Helens, 131-4, 137
Multiverse theory, 39-40, 71
Mutation, 27, 57-8, 60-1, 66-7, 90-1, 108, 134
Naturalism, 27-8
Natural Selection, 11, 60, 65, 77, 87-9, 91, 95, 107, 169
Nautiloids, 121
New creation, 162
Newton, Sir Isaac, 19-20
Niagara Falls, 135-6
Ockham's Razor, 148-9
Old Red Sandstone, 114, 120-1
Oort Cloud, 138
Origin of Species, The, 11, 14, 17, 20, 30, 54
Oxygen, 43, 84
Panspermia, 54, 149
Penrose, Roger, 38, 70, 147, 163
Pentadactyl limbs, 103-4, 109-10
Peppered moths, 11, 75-9, 107

Permafrost, 122
Piltdown Man, 100
Population growth, 143
Proteins, 51-4, 58, 60-2, 65, 87, 104
Punctuated equilibrium, 146
Radiometric dating, 137
Rainbow, 96
Redwall Limestone, 121
Rees, Martin, 33-4, 70, 147
Relativity, Theory of, 20
Rendle-Short, Arthur, 151
Repentance, 158
Resurrection of Jesus, 157, 161-2
Revelation, 157, 159
Rocks, igneous, 115
Rocks, sedimentary, 93, 108, 113-7, 122-4, 129, 132-4, 138
Salinity of seas, 136
Sanskrit, 143
Satan, 159-60
Seas, 21, 44, 47-8, 72, 93, 114, 116, 121, 123, 128, 136, 165
Sedimentation, 113-6
Siberia, 122
Sin, 152, 158, 159, 161
Sinatra, Frank, 158
Singularities, 31
Soup, chemical, 53
Spirit Lake, 131, 133-4
Steady State, Theory of the universe, 12
Suffering, 28, 74, 152, 156, 159-62
Sun, 15, 20-1, 34, 38, 41-2, 44, 47-9, 55, 70, 72, 89, 138, 154, 165
Swamps, 123, 134
Tectonic plates, 115, 128
Theism, 29
Thermodynamics, Second Law of, 89

Toutle River, 131-3

Trees, 11, 19, 21, 70, 88, 114, 119, 122-3, 131, 133-5, 140, 143, 155, 165

Trilobites, 12, 95, 108, 111

Uniformity, Principle of, 113-4, 116-7, 122, 129, 134

Variation, 12, 20, 75, 77-9, 87-8, 90-1, 103, 107, 111, 169

Venus, 43

Volcanism, 115, 124, 128-9

Water, 22, 38, 41-4, 47-50, 55, 70, 79, 90, 93, 114, 119, 121, 123-4, 126-9, 135-6, 155, 165-6

Wheels, 79, 105-6, 110

Whitcomb and Morris, 129, 172

Woolly mammoths, 122

Lightning Source UK Ltd.
Milton Keynes UK
UKOW06f2151041115

262110UK00002B/8/P